REMARKABLE
JEWISH WOMEN

Left to Right
Top Row: Deborah, Golda Meir,
Annie Nathan Meyer, Henrietta Szold

Second Row: Eve, Judith Resnick, Emma Lazarus,
Betty Friedan

Third Row: Rebecca, Bertha Kalich,
Ruth Bader Ginsburg, Sally Preisand

Fourth Row: Amy Eilberg, Vitke Kempner Kovner

REMARKABLE JEWISH WOMEN

Rebels, Rabbis, and Other Women from Biblical Times to the Present

by Emily Taitz and Sondra Henry

The Jewish Publication Society
Philadelphia • Jerusalem

**This book is dedicated to our grandchildren —
those present, and those yet to come**.

Manufactured in the United States of America

Taitz, Emily.

 *Remarkable Jewish women: rebels, rabbis, and other women from biblical
 times to the present / by Emily Taitz and Sondra Henry.*

  p. cm.

 Includes bibliographical references and index.

 *Summary: Presents brief portraits of more than eighty Jewish women and
 introduces the historical, social, and cultural backgrounds of the periods
 during which they lived.*

 ISBN 0-8276-0573-0 [cloth] ISBN 0-8276-0643-5 [paper]

 *1. Jewish women—Biography—Juvenile literature. [1. Jewish women—
 Biography. 2. Women—Biography.] I. Henry, Sondra. II. Title.
 DS 115.2 T34 1996*

 920.72'089924—dc20   *95-51989*

                                                          AC

  RRDC
00 99 98 97 10 9 8 7 6 5 4 3 2

The publication of this book was made possible

through a generous grant from the

MAURICE AMADO FOUNDATION,

whose mission is to perpetuate

Sephardic heritage and culture.

Contents

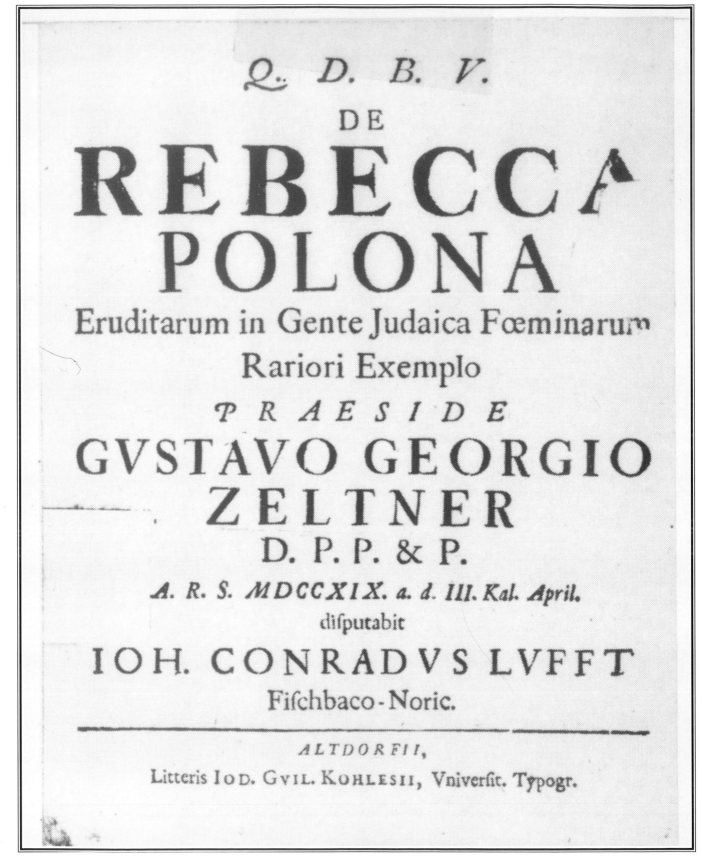

Q. D. B. V.

DE

REBECCA

POLONA

Eruditarum in Gente Judaica Fœminarum

Rariori Exemplo

PRAESIDE

GVSTAVO GEORGIO

ZELTNER

D. P. P. & P.

A. R. S. MDCCXIX. a. d. III. Kal. April.

disputabit

IOH. CONRADVS LVFFT

Fischbaco-Noric.

ALTDORFII,

Litteris Iod. Gvil. Kohlesii, Vniversit. Typogr.

The title page of a book written about Rebecca Tiktiner in 1719.

An Alphabetical Listing
of Remarkable Jewish Women*

*See index for names of other women mentioned in the book.

ACKNOWLEDGMENTS

First and foremost, we would like to thank our editor, Bruce Black, whose careful readings and rereadings helped to perfect this book. Our appreciation also goes to Dr. Ellen Frankel for her thoughtful suggestions and Dr. Judith Baskin who was kind enough to read the manuscript and offer her expert advice.

Doris Gold, always a gold mine of information, was especially instrumental in researching and obtaining the photos used in this book and advising us on research possibilities. We are most thankful for her help and for the photographic services of Hilary Marcus of Impact Visuals.

Thanks also to Dianne Spielman and Wendy Henry of the Leo Baeck Institute, Dina Abramowicz of YIVO, and all the research librarians at the Jewish Theological Seminary Library for their help.

Susan Weidman Schneider, editor of *Lilith* magazine, and Alice Morawetz were also most generous, sharing information and contacts with us whenever we needed it. Rabbi Sue Levi Elwell was kind enough to help us gather new information on Lady Asenath Mizrahi.

Our appreciation to Joy Benjamin, Rita Gordonson, Dr. Edward Henry, Hermine Rubman, and Isaac Taitz for their efforts on behalf of this book. Special thanks to Ari Taitz for helping to guide us through the mysteries of the Internet.

Women, too, were sometimes scholars.

Introduction

Many books about Jewish people tell stories of men who were great scholars, advisers to kings, adventurers, travelers, and traders in jewels and spices. But what about the women?

Women, too, were sometimes scholars, advisers, or successful merchants, but they faced more challenges than men. As with women in the broader society, Jewish women were not trained to be part of public life the way men were.

In traditional Jewish life a woman was expected to marry, run the household, care for the children, and, when necessary, help her husband earn a living. Jewish scholars considered these tasks important enough to excuse women from many of the commandments *(mitzvot)* that men were required to observe. However, Jewish society as a whole tended to value women's activities less than those of men.

The Talmud consists of laws and commentary based on biblical codes and Jewish customs. It sets forth different rules for men and women. In the past, women were only expected to learn the commandments which they had to follow. These included three major laws. One required women to light candles on the eve of every Sabbath and holiday. Another commanded that women separate a portion of the dough when baking challah, in memory of the portion set aside for the priests in the ancient Temple in Jerusalem. The third law involved the observance of ritual purity, which meant that women must keep apart from their husbands during menstruation. They also had to learn how to keep a kosher house (the laws of *kashrut*).

Women usually learned these commandments at home, from their mothers. They were exempt from most ritual observances, scheduled at specific times. A strict schedule of ritual observances might have interfered with household and family duties.

Men, on the other hand, had to know and observe all 613 commandments *(mitzvot)* listed in the Talmud, so they were encouraged and expected to study. Since Jewish culture has always valued learning, scholars were highly honored in the Jewish community, and most scholars were men.

Women usually left legal and religious matters to the men in their families. However, they did participate in many important activities. In addition to preparing the Sabbath loaves, kindling the

Sabbath lights, and observing Jewish laws connected with marriage, they assisted at childbirth and arranged dowries so that poor young women could marry. They cared for the sick, helped orphans and widows, and prepared women after death for burial.

These were the traditional roles, but many women went beyond them. Some performed difficult or brave deeds. Some became scholars. Others had noble qualities or were known for special achievements such as writing poetry, forming new organizations, donating to Jewish causes, and acting as community leaders.

In the past two centuries, as education for girls became accepted, women

Left to right: Top row—Bertha Kalich, Amy Eilberg, Sally Preisand;
Bottom row—Ruth Bader Ginsburg, Judith Hauptman, Vitke Kempner Kovner.

began to find more opportunities in public life. Social changes greatly increased the numbers of outstanding and accomplished women.

The women we have written about in the following pages are only a sample. To find them, we searched through books of Jewish legends, letters, memoirs, and other sources. We tried to include Jewish women from every corner of the world and from many different cultures.

Although all Jews trace their heritage to ancient Israel, our Jewish ancestors began to migrate to other continents early in their history. For a variety of economic, social, and religious reasons, Jews were often forced to leave the places where they settled. Jews from Germany, France, and England (Ashkenazim) tended to immigrate into the nearby lands of Eastern Europe during periods of persecution. Spanish Jews (Sephardim) who were expelled from Spain in 1492 scattered to such diverse countries as Holland, Turkey, and Italy. Others fled to North Africa or back to the Middle East. The Sephardim and Ashkenazim became culturally different as time went on; both groups produced many remarkable women.

In this book, we have tried to choose women who acted out of moral courage and with unselfish motives, as well as those who made important contributions in other ways. It was impossible to include them all. If we have left out one of your favorite heroines, we invite you to tell us about her. Perhaps she can be included in a future edition of this book.

Come with us now as we meet and learn about great women: the scholars, leaders, rebels, and heroines in our history.

Eve in the garden, as envisioned by a nineteenth century artist.

Chapter 1

A New Look at Old Stories

Bible stories come down to us from a long time ago. Some may be four thousand years old or older. They tell us a great deal about the lands of the Middle East, the people who lived there, and what they believed. These stories present both women and men as complex individuals who sometimes act in ways that may seem unfair. However, stories from the Bible can show us how women dealt with difficult situations. From the Bible we learn how our ancestors built the nation of Israel from a single family.

Eve

In Chapters 1 and 2 of Genesis, the first book of the Hebrew Bible, we read that God created Adam and Eve; they were the first human beings on earth. God placed them in a beautiful garden which provided them with all the food they needed. In the Garden of Eden, Eve and Adam enjoyed eternal life. God imposed only one rule on them: they were forbidden to eat the fruit of the "tree of the knowledge of good and evil."

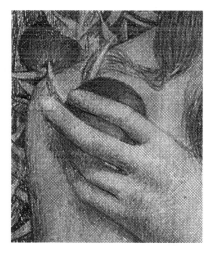

Into this perfect paradise came the serpent, the most cunning of all the animals. He tried to convince Eve to eat the forbidden fruit. At first, Eve hesitated, remembering God's command. But gradually, the serpent tempted her by suggesting "that the tree was desirable as a source of wisdom."

Eve made a choice. She ate some of the fruit and then persuaded Adam to eat some too. When God discovered how Eve and Adam had disobeyed, God banished them from the Garden. From that moment on, Eve, and every woman after her, would suffer pain during childbirth. Adam, and every man after him, would have to work for a living "by the sweat of his brow." Eve and Adam became like all human beings are today. They would no longer live forever.

Eve is usually blamed for what happened in the Garden of Eden, but she had made an important decision — the first human decision recorded in the Bible. She chose knowledge over obedience.

THE FOUR MOTHERS

When we talk about the four Mothers, we mean the biblical women Sarah, Rebecca, Rachel, and Leah. These important women were the female heads of the original Israelite families; they are considered the mothers of the Jewish people. Abraham, Isaac, and Jacob are referred to as the fathers of our people.

Sarah

The name Sarah means "princess." Sarah was the wife of Abraham. He was the first person to believe in one God. According to tradition, when Abraham taught the men about God, Sarah taught the women. Together, they convinced others to believe in God and come with them to the land of Canaan.

Sarah and Abraham wanted a child, but Sarah did not become pregnant, even after many years of marriage. When she realized that she was too old to bear children, she offered her servant, Hagar, to Abraham for a second wife. This may sound strange to us today, but in Sarah's time it was accepted. Men sometimes had more than one wife, and some women had control over their personal servants. These "maidservants," as they are known in the Bible, had no legal rights of their own. Because Hagar was owned by Sarah, if she gave birth to a child, the child would belong to Sarah.

Hagar did have a son named Ishmael. Shortly after his birth, three angels from God came to visit Abraham in his tent. Sarah overheard the angels promise her husband that she would bear a son. She laughed when she heard this because she was 90 years old and no longer able to have children. When the angels' prediction came true, and Sarah had a son, Abraham and Sarah named him Isaac, from the Hebrew word for laughter.

As Isaac grew up, Sarah became resentful of Hagar and Ishmael. She demanded that Abraham send them away. She reminded Abraham that Isaac was his rightful heir and would become the leader of the people who believed in one God.

Sarah's demand upset Abraham, but God spoke directly to him and instructed him to listen to his wife. God said: ". . . it is through Isaac that offspring shall be continued for you." Abraham obeyed God and sent Hagar and Ishmael away. God took care of them in the desert, and Ishmael came to be acknowledged as the father of the Arab people. Through her determination and acceptance of God's will, Sarah became the first mother of Israel.

Rebecca meeting Eliezer at the well, drawn by a nineteenth century artist.

Rebecca

When Isaac became older, Abraham sent his servant, Eliezer, to his ancestral home at Paddan-Aram, a city north of Canaan, to search for a bride for Isaac. Eliezer asked God to give him a sign that would help him recognize the woman worthy to be Isaac's wife.

Fourteen-year-old Rebecca, the daughter of Abraham's kinsman Bethuel, was approaching the spring to water her father's camels when she saw Eliezer. He asked her for some water and Rebecca offered him a drink from her own jug. Then she helped him water his camels. This was the sign Eliezer had asked for. He was impressed with her thoughtfulness and generosity. When he learned that Rebecca was Abraham's niece, Eliezer was sure this was the wife God intended for his master's son. Abraham had specifically commanded Eliezer

to "get a wife for my son from my kindred, from my father's house."

Rebecca brought Eliezer to her home to meet her family. Her father and brother received him warmly. When they discovered the reason for his visit, the men discussed it among themselves and approved of the marriage. Following the custom of the time, Eliezer then gave Rebecca many valuable gifts from Abraham's family. However, final agreement had to come from Rebecca herself.

"Will you go with this man?" her father and brother asked.

Rebecca answered: "I will."

This simple exchange established a tradition that no Jewish woman could be forced to marry; she must marry of her own free will.

When Rebecca met Isaac, he brought her to the tent of his mother, Sarah, who had died some time before. Rebecca took over the female role of leadership within the family.

It took many years for Rebecca to become pregnant. During her pregnancy, she had a dream in which God spoke to her. "Two nations are in your womb," God said. "One people shall be mightier than the other, and the older shall serve the younger." To Rebecca, this meant that the younger of the two boys would inherit the leadership of the family.

Rebecca did give birth to twin sons. The first was named Esau, and the second, who followed a few minutes later, was called Jacob. Rebecca preferred Jacob, because he was gentle, intelligent, and sensitive. Isaac preferred the first-born, Esau, because he was a good fighter and loved to hunt.

Isaac wanted Esau to inherit his land and flocks as well as the leadership of the family. Rebecca, however, had been told by God in her dream that the elder son would serve the younger. She believed that Jacob was destined to be the leader, and she had the courage to act on that conviction.

When Isaac was old and blind, Rebecca heard him send Esau hunting. Isaac wanted Esau to prepare his favorite meat. After he ate, Isaac planned to give Esau a special blessing.

Rebecca waited for Esau to leave and then told Jacob to get two goats from the flock and slaughter them. She cooked some goat stew and had Jacob bring it to his father. Before he went in, Rebecca put the hairy goatskin on Jacob's hands so his skin would feel rough like his brother's.

From the smell of the food and the touch of his hands, Isaac thought that it was Esau. He gave Jacob the special blessing reserved for the firstborn son and bestowed on him the leadership of the family. Only after Esau arrived and asked for his father's blessing did Isaac realize he had already granted this blessing to Jacob. Once given, however, he could not take it back. He gave Esau a different blessing, promising him prosperity even though he would have to serve his younger brother.

Soon after, when Jacob set off to find a wife in Paddan-Aram, Isaac blessed him again, repeating the blessing of leadership. Despite his first preference for Esau, Isaac now recognized, as Rebecca had, that it was Jacob whom God intended to carry on the heritage of Abraham. Although Rebecca had deceived Isaac, she did it in order to fulfill God's will.

Rachel and Leah

Jacob went to Paddan-Aram to seek a wife from his mother's family, just as his father, Isaac, had done. He saw his cousin Rachel coming to water her flocks at the well. Rachel was very beautiful and Jacob fell in love with her as soon as he saw her.

A marriage was arranged between Jacob and Rachel, and Rachel gave her consent. Jacob promised to work for Laban, Rachel's father, for seven years. After that time, Rachel would marry Jacob.

When Jacob had worked for seven years, Laban had a wedding feast prepared. The bride was led into the darkened wedding tent. Without Jacob's knowledge, Laban substituted his older daughter, Leah, for Rachel. Laban later excused this deception by explaining that it was custom for the older daughter to be married first.

Rachel tending her

father's sheep.

The following morning, when he realized his bride was not Rachel, Jacob was furious. Laban calmed him, promising him that he could marry Rachel also. In biblical times, men often had more than one wife. Laban kept his word this time, but Jacob had to agree to work for his father-in-law for seven more years.

After their marriage, both sisters were anxious to have many children. Leah had four sons but Rachel had none. In their attempts to produce larger families, both Leah and Rachel did just what Sarah had done. Rachel gave Jacob her personal servant, Bilhah, as an additional wife. Leah gave Jacob her servant Zilpah for the same purpose. Both Bilhah and Zilpah had children. Jacob fathered ten sons and one daughter, Dinah. But Rachel, the wife he loved the best, was still childless.

Rachel begged God to grant her a child. She complained to Jacob: "Give me children or I shall die." Finally, quite late in life, God answered Rachel's prayers. She bore two sons: Joseph and Benjamin. Rachel died giving birth to Benjamin and was buried in Bethlehem, a town east of Jerusalem.

There are many legends telling of Rachel's kindness, compassion, and love. One of these legends relates that hundreds of years after her death, when the Israelites were led into exile, they passed near her grave and cried out to her. Rachel heard their plea and asked God for compassion on behalf of her descendants. God promised Rachel that her people would eventually return from exile.

Even today, Jews still visit Rachel's grave and offer special prayers. They believe that because of her own suffering she will understand their needs and ask God to grant their wishes.

All Jacob's twelve sons married and raised their own families. These families became the twelve tribes of Israel, since Jacob was also known by the name Israel. The Bible traces their lineage through their fathers, Abraham, Isaac, and Jacob. However, it was the choices and decisions of the four mothers, Sarah, Rebecca, Rachel, and Leah, that shaped the leadership and the fate of the Jewish people.

Miriam

Miriam, along with her brothers, Moses and Aaron, was a great leader. Her story is included in the biblical Book of Exodus, and parts of it are retold every Passover.

Even when she was very young, Miriam was considered to be a prophet. That means that God spoke through her. According to tradition, she predicted the birth of a brother who would grow up to save Israel. That brother was Moses.

When the Hebrews (as the Israelites were called then) lived in Egypt, the Pharaoh, supreme ruler of all Egypt, decided that they were becoming too numerous. He made a rule that all baby boys born to Hebrew women had to be killed immediately. This terrible law caused much suffering and sadness.

Two heroic women of that period were Shifrah and Puah, the only midwives mentioned by name in the Book of Exodus. Their job was to help the Hebrew women deliver their babies. The Egyptian rulers ordered Shifrah and Puah to kill the boy babies as soon as they were born. These two brave women refused to obey. Even though it was against the law they continued their work and saved every child.

Miriam rejoiced with the Hebrew women after crossing the Red Sea.

Miriam's mother had just given birth to a baby boy. Miriam knew that the family couldn't hide him for long. Using branches and mud, she helped her mother, Yocheved, make a little basket. With the baby inside, she and Yocheved placed the basket among the reeds in the Nile River. Miriam watched as the Pharaoh's daughter, Bithiah, discovered the baby and pulled him from the river. Then Miriam rushed forward and offered to find a nurse for him.

Pharaoh's daughter agreed, and Miriam brought her mother to nurse the baby. He was named Moses, a name that means "drawn out of the water." Moses was raised in the royal court, but because of Miriam, Yocheved had the opportunity to care for her son in his early years. When Moses grew up, he answered God's call and led the Hebrews out of slavery in Egypt.

After the Israelites crossed the Red Sea, Miriam, playing on a tambourine, joyfully led all the Hebrew women in a song of thanks to God. The verse in the Book of Exodus says: "And Miriam the prophetess . . . took a timbrel in her hand; and all the women went out after her . . . ."

Miriam wandered in the desert with the children of Israel for many years. According to legend, a well followed Miriam, providing water for the Israelites. Tradition says the well was Miriam's reward for protecting her baby brother while he was in the river Nile.

Miriam died before the Israelites reached the promised land. After her death, they had no water for many days. The lack of water symbolizes her people's loss following the death of this great leader.

Deborah was

a judge and

prophet in Israel.

Deborah

Long after the ancient Hebrews left Egypt to return to the Promised Land, another prophet appeared to lead the people. She was one of the great heroines of the Bible: "Deborah the wife of Lappidot."

During Deborah's lifetime, the Israelite tribes were still not united. The neighboring Canaanites took advantage of this lack of unity. They attacked the tribes separately and succeeded in making life difficult and dangerous. The Israelites knew they must protect themselves. It was hard for them to grow their crops and take care of their families because they always had to fight. What they needed was a strong leader. Together, the Israelite tribes could drive the Canaanites away.

The Bible tells us that Deborah was a prophet "who led Israel at that time." The people came to her for decisions and judgments. God commanded Deborah to send an army against the Canaanites and promised a victory. As a woman, though, Deborah was not trained to fight. She summoned the warrior Barak and told him of God's command. She asked him to lead ten thousand Israelites against the Canaanite army of Sisera.

Barak was afraid. The Canaanites had horses, weapons of iron, and chariots to help them fight. The Israelites had none of these things. Yet he could not refuse Deborah's request. He said: "If you will go with me, then I will go."

Deborah agreed to accompany Barak into battle. But she warned him that he would not gain any honor fighting the Canaanites. Nor would he succeed in killing General Sisera. Instead, Deborah predicted: "The Lord will give Sisera into the hand of a woman."

These words proved to be true. Although Barak's army did win the war, Sisera ran away. He came to a tent where a woman named Yael was living. Yael was neither a Canaanite nor an Israelite. She belonged to a different tribe that was friendly with Israel.

When Yael saw Sisera running from the battle, she invited him to rest in her tent. She gave him milk to drink and waited until he fell asleep. Then she killed him with a tent peg. This brave deed helped to guarantee peace for the Israelite tribes.

Deborah's song of victory is included in the biblical Book of Judges. It is one of the few poems written by a woman which became part of the Bible. In it, Deborah praises God, but she also praises herself. She reminds the Israelites: "Deliverance ceased . . . in Israel, till you arose, O Deborah . . . O mother in Israel."

Deborah also has a special place for Yael in her song. She describes how Yael killed Sisera and said: "Most blessed of women [shall] be Yael . . . ."

Deborah is the only woman who led all the people of ancient Israel in both war and peace. She encouraged the twelve tribes to gather together and help protect each other. After Deborah's victory, the Israelites enjoyed forty years of peace.

Yael killed General Sisera with a tent peg.

Hannah

Hannah's story is told in the Book of Samuel I. She was one of the two wives of Elkanah. Elkanah's other wife, Penina, bore many children but Hannah was childless. This made her very unhappy, even though she was Elkanah's favorite wife. Hannah decided that when the family made its yearly trip to the House of the Lord at Shiloh, she would ask God for a child.

After the traditional sacrifices to God and a festive meal, Hannah remained behind. She found a quiet corner, and with her lips moving but her voice silent, she prayed for a son.

Individual, personal prayer was not common practice among ancient Israelites. When Eli, the high priest, saw Hannah praying without making a sound, he accused her of being drunk. Hannah told Eli that she certainly was not drunk, but was pouring out her heart to God in silent devotion.

Hannah promised God that if she gave birth to a son, her son would serve God for his whole life. Less than a year later, Hannah's first child was born. She named him Samuel which means "God has heard."

As Sarah and Rebecca had done before her, Hannah, too, determined the future of her child. When Samuel was old enough, she brought him to the House of the Lord at Shiloh just as she had promised. Under the care of the high priest Eli, Samuel was to learn God's laws.

Before she left her son at Shiloh, Hannah prayed once more. This time, her prayer expressed her great joy and gratitude to God for granting her a son. Her inspired words are included in the Bible as an example of personal prayer.

Hannah had three more sons and two daughters, but only Samuel was destined to be a prophet. Hannah is a model of faith and devotion, and the mother of one of the great leaders of Israel.

Ruth

Ruth lived in the land of Moab, east of Bethlehem, beyond the Dead Sea. Her people were not Israelites and did not observe the laws of Moses. She married the son of Naomi, an Israelite widow. After ten years of marriage, Ruth's husband died. Ruth remained in Naomi's household with Orpah, her sister-in-law. Orpah and Ruth had much in common. Orpah's family were not Israelites, either, and Orpah had also lost her husband.

When their mother-in-law, Naomi, decided to return to her home in Bethlehem, she urged Orpah and Ruth to stay with their own people. Orpah reluctantly remained behind in Moab. Ruth refused to stay behind. She said to her mother-in-law: "Do not urge me to leave you . . . For wherever you go, I will go . . . Your people will be my people, and your God [will be] my God."

Ruth's loyalty toward her husband's people went beyond family ties. With this statement she formally identified herself as an Israelite. Ruth left her mother and father and the only land she had known. A stranger in a strange land, she courageously faced poverty and uncertainty to accept the God of the Israelites.

Arriving in Bethlehem at harvest time, Ruth gathered ears of grain that the reapers dropped. This was in keeping with the biblical law which provided for poor people who had no land of their own. Because of this law, Ruth was able to collect food for herself and her mother-in-law.

The field where she chose to work belonged to Boaz, a relative of Naomi. As Naomi's relative, Boaz had specific obligations to Ruth. Biblical law required that Boaz marry the wife of his kinsman if she had no children. This would guarantee the continuation of the family line.

With Naomi's guidance, Ruth married Boaz. Together, they had a son named Obed, the grandfather of King David.

The story of Ruth illustrates the importance of each individual in Jewish tradition. King David, the greatest and most beloved king of Israel, descended from Ruth, a convert to Judaism.

Because *Megillat* (the scroll, or book of) Ruth takes place during harvest time, we read the Book of Ruth on Shavuot, a harvest holiday.

Ruth followed Naomi into Israel while Orpah returned to Moab.

Esther

Esther was a beautiful, young Jewish woman who lived in Persia over two thousand years ago. When Ahasuerus, King of Persia, chose Esther to be his wife, he selected her from among many fair maidens in the land. As Queen, she went to live with all the other wives of the king. She took her place in the women's quarters of the palace in Shushan, the capital of Persia.

Queen Esther and King Ahasuerus pictured on their thrones, from a third century mural.

Esther's cousin Mordecai, who was also her guardian, warned her not to reveal her Jewish origins to the king. Even though many Jews lived in Persia, they were a foreign minority and regarded with suspicion by the Persians.

One of King Ahasuerus's most trusted advisors was a man named Haman. Haman hated the Jews and convinced King Ahasuerus to issue an order to destroy "a certain people . . . whose laws are different . . . and do not obey the king's laws."

Esther learned about this terrible plan and sent a messenger to Mordecai. The messenger returned with Mordecai's instructions. Esther was to go before the king to "appeal to him and to plead with him for her people."

Esther knew that to approach the king without his permission could mean death for anyone, even a royal wife, but she was willing to take the risk. She told Mordecai to ask the Jews to pray and fast for three days. Esther had heard that women whom the king favored could receive special treatment for their people.

On the third day, dressed in her royal robes, Esther appeared unannounced in the king's court. When King Ahasuerus saw Esther, he held out his scepter to her and invited her to approach the throne. All she wanted, Esther told the king, was to invite Ahasuerus and his advisor Haman to a great feast.

At the banquet, after the men had drunk their wine, Esther told the king of Haman's plot. She explained how Haman planned to kill all the Jewish people and finally admitted that she, too, was a Jew.

King Ahasuerus was furious with Haman and ordered him put to death. Official letters were sent throughout the land permitting the Jews to resist and defend themselves against any attack. After Haman's death and the victory of the Jews over their enemies, Queen Esther called for a great day of feasting and celebration.

When Esther first came to the palace, she did not know she would have to carry out an important and dangerous mission. However, she had the strength and courage to meet the challenge. Because of her bravery, Jewish tradition recalls these events in *Megillat* (the scroll of) Esther and we remember them every year on the holiday of Purim.

Ruth and Esther are the only women who have entire, individual books of the Bible written about them. Most modern scholars think that these books are not based on fact. However, they are wonderful stories about heroic women. Real or not, these women have become an important part of the Jewish tradition.

Judith cutting off the head of Holofernes.

Chapter 2

Ancient Clues

Jews continued to live in their "Holy Land" long after biblical times. Following the death of King Solomon, the son of David, they broke up into two Israelite nations: Israel, the northern kingdom, and Judah in the south. Israel was destroyed in 722 B.C.E. and its inhabitants driven out. This left Judah as the only Israelite nation of the Middle East. It is from the name Judah (Judea in Latin) that the words "Jew" and "Jewish" are derived.

Many Jewish books have been written since the Bible. Ancient books recorded the ideas of people who lived after Biblical times. Some of these writings were gathered into a collection called the Apocrypha. This is a Greek word meaning "hidden away" or "unknown." Unlike the writings that make up the Bible, these writings were not considered holy books by the Jews. Therefore they were not saved as carefully or respected as much by Jewish tradition.

Among the best-known stories included in the Apocrypha are the four books of the Maccabees and the Book of Judith. The books of the Maccabees recount the history and legends surrounding the holiday of Hanukkah. These events occurred in the first century B.C.E., about six hundred years after the northern kingdom was destroyed. Although the most famous heroes of Hanukkah are the five Maccabean brothers, there were heroic women during this period. One of them was Judith.

Judith

Judith was a beautiful, rich young widow who led a quiet life in the northern border town of Betulia. She went out very little and spent no time with men although she was much admired.

When the Assyrian army, led by General Holofernes, laid siege to the town, the people of Betulia were frightened and worried. They did not have a large army to protect them, nor did they have a strong leader among the elders of their community. Seeing the concern among the townspeople, Judith decided to act.

She dressed herself in her loveliest clothes, and with the permission of the town elders, she walked down to where the army was camped. As she had hoped, Holofernes saw her. He was attracted first by her beauty, then by her intelligence and wit. He invited her to dine with him that night and she accepted, bringing her maid with her.

During the banquet in his tent, Holofernes drank too much wine. Never suspecting that his charming dinner guest would harm him, he fell asleep. Judith had waited for just this moment. She took the general's own sword in her hands and, with a mighty blow, cut off his head. She handed the grisly trophy of war to her maid and the two women returned in triumph to their village.

With their leader beheaded, the Assyrian army had no heart to fight and ran away. Betulia was saved by Judith's brave deeds.

Many people believe that the Book of Judith, like the Books of Ruth and Esther, is a historical novel. Some scholars suggest that the Book of Judith was written during the time of the Maccabees to give people courage. However, Judith has long been counted as a heroine of her people. Her deeds have been retold in operas, poems, and novels in many different languages. Famous paintings show Judith and her maid returning with the head of Holofernes. She is remembered by Jews each year during Hanukkah because, like the Maccabees, she risked her life for her people.

THE WOMEN OF THE TALMUD

Jewish settlements spread beyond the borders of the ancient Israelite nation, but Judah remained a center of Jewish life until the first few centuries of the common era (C.E.). The great Jewish leaders lived and taught in Judah and in the Galilee, an area further to the north. Their discussions were recorded in the Talmud, one of the most important compilations of law and teaching that the Jewish people ever produced.

Jewish scholars of this period were almost all men, but some stories about women did find their way into the Talmud. There were even a few rare occasions when women's opinions were quoted by the male sages.

Ima Shalom

Ima Shalom is one woman whose words and deeds are recorded in the Talmud. Born in Palestine in 50 C.E., long before the Talmud was put together, she appears in a number of talmudic stories.

Ima Shalom belonged to a distinguished family. First her father and then her brother headed the Sanhedrin, the Jewish governing body that made important decisions for the Jews of the area. Her husband, Eliezer ben Hyrcanus, was a great scholar. Ima Shalom was known for her intellect, her outspoken manner, and her wise sayings.

Her husband insisted that "woman's place is at the spinning wheel," but he certainly could not keep his wife there. She often participated in the men's discussions.

"All gates are closed except the gates of wounded feelings," Ima Shalom once said. She meant that God will always hear the prayers of those who have been wronged.

In another clever comment attributed to Ima Shalom, the Talmud tells of her conversation with an emperor who challenged the Jews concerning their God.

"Your God is a thief," he said, "because he stole a rib from Adam."

Ima Shalom is said to have answered: "Last night a robber broke into my house and carried away some silver vessels leaving gold ones in their place."

"I wish such a robber visited my house every night!" the emperor responded.

"This is what happened to Adam," she informed him. "God took a rib from him and gave him a wife in its place."

Beruriah

Beruriah lived almost one hundred years after Ima Shalom. She was involved in learned discussions in her father's home when she was quite young. When she grew up, she married Rabbi Meir, an important scholar.

Meir and Beruriah lived with their twin sons in the northern part of Palestine. Meir participated in the sessions of the Palestinian academy (yeshivah) and taught others to read and understand Jewish laws.

Beruriah was also known for her wisdom and was considered a model of dedication and scholarship. One story relates that Beruriah "studied three hundred laws from three hundred teachers each day."

Beruriah had her own pupils and was a demanding instructor. She clearly explained the important and meaningful parts of Jewish law. One day, Beruriah overheard Meir praying for the death of some thieves who had been causing trouble in the neighborhood. She reminded him that the law does not say "let sinners cease;" it says "let sins cease." She taught that we should not pray for the death of sinners, but for their repentance.

The most famous legend about Beruriah illustrates her complete faith in God. When her two sons were taken ill and died suddenly, she explained this tragic event to her husband by asking: "Someone has lent me two jewels and now he wants them back. Should I return them?"

When Meir replied that she certainly must return the jewels, Beruriah revealed the deaths of the children and said: "Did you not say we must return to the owner the precious jewels he entrusted to us?" Beruriah accepted the deaths of her sons because she believed the children came from God and must be returned to God.

Beruriah is a rare example of a learned woman of her time. She had the ability to interpret the Torah, and the courage to express her opinions. Because of these strengths, she is the only woman whose words became talmudic law.

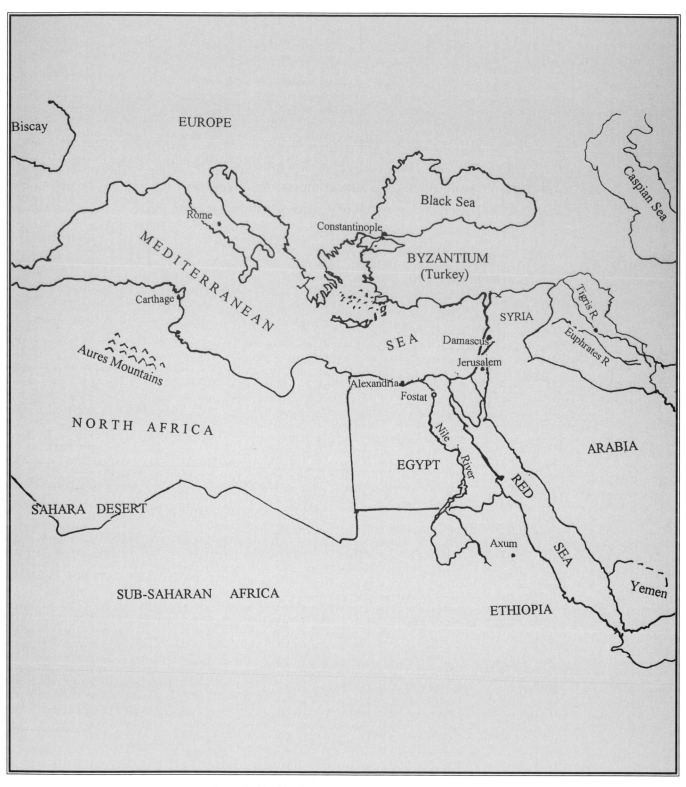

Jews who lived in these areas were organized into tribes.

Chapter 3

Out of the Desert

The lives of some women are so shrouded in the mists of the past that their deeds have remained largely undocumented. This is especially true where record-keeping was haphazard. Without records, it is almost impossible to know very much about a community or its members. Over the centuries, much of women's history has been lost.

A few women, however, live on in fragments of ancient books, or in legends from the past. Their lives can never be fully reconstructed, but we can use the few facts we do know to broaden our knowledge of Jewish women.

Even after the establishment of the Muslim religion in the seventh century, the people of North Africa, Saudi Arabia, and Yemen, including the Jews, were organized into tribes. Each tribe practiced its own religion, but all the tribes valued prowess in war. The prestige of a person or a tribe depended on success in warfare. This was true of Jewish as well as Christian, Muslim, or pagan tribes.

Such standards may seem unusual to contemporary Jews, who often think of the Jewish people in those early centuries as defenseless and persecuted. Most people believe that the Jews condemned war, and after the destruction of the land of Israel, never had an army; but through the lives of a few women who lived in the seventh, eighth, and tenth centuries we discover a different aspect of our history. We also learn about Jews who lived in remote corners of the world, far away from mainstream Jewish communities.

One of the ways we learn about these women is through old poems. Among the Arabian Jewish tribes, poetry was a time-honored way of preserving the past. Women composed verses praising the exploits of their tribal chiefs and recalling heroic battles. Fragments of their work can still be found more than a thousand years later.

Scattered through old records and poems we also discover scraps of information about women who were warriors. They sometimes fought alongside the men and on rare occasions led all-male armies. Their deeds of heroism may not fit our standards. Their bravery, however, deserves recognition. These women warriors followed in the footsteps of the prophet Deborah, the heroine Yael, and the daring Judith who killed Holofernes.

Sarah of Yemen

Sarah was a poet who lived in Yemen, an area directly south of Saudi Arabia, during the time of Muhammad (570-632 C.E.). Many Yemenite Jews were oral poets. The art of poetry has been practiced by Yemenite women well into the twentieth century. These women would recite Hebrew quotations from classical poems and stories. They combined them with love songs and reports of political events, creating a unique and personal style.

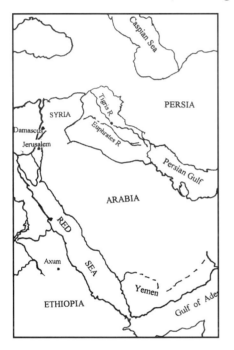

Some Yemenite women poets may not even have known how to read or write. However, their poems and songs were memorized and passed orally from one generation to another. Composed in the Arabic language, a few were eventually written down by early historians and researchers. Sarah's poem has been preserved, perhaps because it deals with the history of the B'nai Quraiza, a strong and influential Jewish tribe.

Before 620 C.E., the year Muhammad established the Muslim faith, the Arab peoples practiced many different religions. Most believed in many gods, but some of the tribes in that area were Christian or Jewish. The Jewish tribes were respected. They often attempted to convince pagans or Christians to accept Judaism. Occasionally they were successful.

Almost one hundred years before Sarah lived, the Jews had converted the Yemenite king Abu Karib and his entire army to Judaism. There is general agreement that his son, Zurak Dhu Nuwas, was an observant Jew. Dhu Nuwas took the Hebrew name of Joseph and ruled all of Yemen from 520 to 530 C.E. During those ten years, many Yemenites became Jews and remained Jewish even after the fall of King Joseph.

While Yemen was a Jewish kingdom, the Jewish tribes who lived nearby, in southern Arabia, became powerful. One of the most powerful was the B'nai Quraiza.

Sarah's poem relates how a Christian tribe first killed the Quraiza chiefs by deceit and trickery. Weakened by the murder of their leaders, the Quraiza were then conquered by another tribe. Finally, they were completely destroyed by

Muhammad, the new religious leader of the Arabian people, in 627 C.E. He first defeated them in battle, then killed all the men and sold the women in exchange for weapons.

Only a fragment of Sarah's poem still remains. It is included in an Arabic collection of ancient literature. However, it is clear that she originally composed her poem as a memorial to this proud Jewish tribe, and as a lament for its destruction:

> *By my life, there is a people not long in Du Hurud, obliterated by the wind.*
>
> *Men of Quraiza destroyed by . . . swords and lances.*
>
> *We have lost, and our loss is so grave, it embitters for its people the pure water,*
>
> *And had they been foreseeing, a teeming host would have reached there before them.*

Was Sarah herself a member of the B'nai Quraiza? No one really knows. According to legend, Sarah was a warrior who fought against Muhammad and was murdered by a follower of the new Muslim religion. However, her poetry, not her courage as a warrior, has preserved her name in history.

Princess Dahiyah Kahina

West of the deserts of Arabia, in the Aurès Mountains of North Africa (presently part of southeastern Algeria), lived other Jewish tribes. They followed the rules of the Sabbath and observed the festivals of the Jewish calendar, as did the Arabian Jewish tribes. They lived among the native tribes, called Berbers, and spoke the Berber language. Both Jews and Berbers were semi-nomadic farmers and warriors. They moved their camps with the seasons, growing some crops and migrating to feed their flocks.

In the seventh century Princess Dahiyah Kahina led the strongest of these Jewish tribes, the Jerawa (commonly known as the Kahina tribe). Dahiyah Kahina's full name was Dahiyah *bint* (daughter of) Thabita *ibn* (son of) Kahina.

The word *Kahina* was once thought to derive from the Hebrew word *Kohen*. However, most scholars now believe it is an old Arabic word meaning soothsayer. This may be the reason why Kahina is often credited with being a prophet who could foretell the future. Nothing is known of Dahiyah Kahina's husband, but stories and legends indicate she had two sons.

While Kahina was the tribal leader, Prince Hassan of Egypt came west with an army. His goal was to conquer the area for the Muslim followers of Muhammad.

Hassan had already won a victory at Carthage in 687 C.E. (Carthage is situated in modern-day Tunisia). Traveling west, his scouts told him that the Kahina tribe was the largest and most powerful in the region. If he could destroy this tribe he would control all of North Africa. In an effort to prevent this, Kahina united Jewish, Christian, and pagan Berber tribes. She led them into battle and defeated Hassan's army.

After the victory, Kahina became queen of western North Africa (*Maghreb* in Arabic) and ruled for five years. Those five years were the longest period of time that this region was united under one leader — until the twentieth century.

After five years, the Muslims struck again. Dahiyah Kahina, accompanied by her sons and the warriors of many tribes, bravely confronted the superior Muslim troops once more. This time her forces could not resist the siege and were defeated. Kahina was seriously wounded and died on the battlefield.

As she lay dying beside a well, Kahina summoned her two sons. She urged them to surrender to Prince Hassan and save their lives. They took their mother's advice and became soldiers in the Arab army. The well, named *Bir al Kahina* (the well of Kahina), still exists in this region. It is said to mark the place where Princess Kahina died.

Judith of Ethiopia

Judith lived in the tenth century in Ethiopia. Like Dahiyah Kahina, Judith was a Jewish warrior queen.

Jewish legends trace a Jewish presence in Ethiopia from the time of the biblical king, Solomon, who reigned from 967 to 928 B.C.E.. According to the Bible (Kings I, Chapter 10) the Queen of Sheba came to visit King Solomon to test his wisdom and see his great wealth. The land of Sheba is believed to have included the lands of Yemen and Ethiopia, separated only by a narrow strait of water at the southern end of the Red Sea.

The Book of Kings does not relate that Solomon and the Queen of Sheba ever married. However, many legends that developed from the original Bible story claim that the two had a son named Menelik.

According to legend, Prince Menelik was raised in Jerusalem, but after the queen's death he returned to Sheba to take possession of his mother's lands. A group of Jews from Solomon's palace accompanied him and settled in his kingdom. Judith claimed descent from this line, establishing that she originated from a noble Jewish family.

By the beginning of the common era, Yemen and Ethiopia had become separate kingdoms, but Yemenite-Arabian influence remained strong in Ethiopia. After the defeat of the Yemenite Jewish king Joseph (Dhu Nuwas) by Ethiopian Christians in the middle of the sixth century C.E.,

Yemenite Jews fled into the Christian kingdom of Ethiopia. Some came as slaves; others came as exiles. The small Jewish population of Ethiopia grew.

By the tenth century, approximately 400 years later, Ethiopian Jews, who called themselves "The House of Israel," had become numerous. They lived together in the northern region and were politically independent. When Queen Judith came to power, she combined her troops with those of other local tribes who were rebelling against the Christian government and marched against the king.

Judith and her rebel army overthrew the Christian king and destroyed churches and monasteries. For forty years Judith — called "the fire" in African legends — rallied her armies and fought the Ethiopian Christians, burning their holy city of Axum. Did Judith herself actually fight, or did she inspire her armies by her leadership? Did Judith have children who continued to lead the Jews of Ethiopia? Neither the details of Judith's life and death nor the reasons for her attack are known, but stories about the warrior queen of Ethiopia have persisted. They remind us that far away in Eastern Africa brave Jewish women lived and died for their people.

Following the rebellion, a new Christian regime took over in Ethiopia. The Ethiopian Jews, because of their power, maintained their semi-independent status and were not persecuted. After three centuries of peace, however, a stronger Christian dynasty was established in the thirteenth century. The new government put an end to Jewish independence in Ethiopia.

A modern descendent

of the ancient

Ethiopian Jews.

Referred to as Falashas (from a word meaning exiles or wanderers), these once strong, proud, and prosperous Jews were deprived of property rights and became impoverished. After suffering many centuries of persecution and isolation from mainstream Judaism, the descendants of Judith have been recognized as Jews by the rabbis of Israel and rescued. With the help of Jews from all over the world, most of the Falashas were flown to Israel and have settled throughout the land. Today they are learning the customs of modern Judaism.

Fragments from the Cairo Geniza were brought back and stored at Cambridge University.

Chapter 4

A Hiding Place in Cairo

Geniza is the Hebrew word for hiding place. This word is often used to refer to one small storeroom in the Ibn Ezra Synagogue in Fostat, Egypt. In this room, from 900 to 1250 C.E., thousands of pieces of paper — letters, documents, court records, and reports — were preserved.

It has always been the custom in Jewish law to bury any paper that contained the name of God rather than to burn or otherwise destroy it. This was a sign of respect. From the tenth through the thirteenth centuries, a time of great faith among Jews, almost every written document contained a reference to God's name. As a result, huge piles of documents accumulated in the storeroom, awaiting burial.

Solomon Schechter examining documents from the Cairo Geniza at Cambridge University.

As time went on, most Jews left Fostat for the new city of Cairo. The old storeroom of the Ibn Ezra Synagogue, with its treasure of old letters and papers, remained locked, awaiting rediscovery.

As the centuries passed, the storeroom was forgotten. Although known to a few scholars and specialists, nothing was done about it until the 1890s when two English sisters, Agnes Lewis and Margaret Gibson, traveled to Egypt. They brought back some of the crumbling letters and showed them to Solomon Schechter, a Jewish scholar at Cambridge University.

Professor Schechter soon realized the importance of these documents to Jewish history. He received permission from Cairo to bring more than 100,000 manuscripts and fragments to England. From that time until today, historians and archaeological experts have been deciphering and studying the papers of the Cairo *Geniza.*

From the *Geniza* documents we learn how ordinary women and men lived, what they thought, and what they did. Women whose lives might never have been recorded in history books are revealed in these ancient letters and records. One of them was a woman named Wuhsha.

Wuhsha

In a time when women in Muslim countries rarely left the confines of their homes, a few Jewish women attempted to gain more personal freedom. They struggled against accepted custom in order to achieve economic and social independence. This effort sometimes led them outside the bounds of accepted Jewish behavior.

Karima (the "dear one"), nicknamed Wuhsha the Broker, was such a woman. Some tantalizing fragments of her life emerge from five separate documents rescued from the Cairo *Geniza.* Although there are many women mentioned in *Geniza* records, Wuhsha is by far the most colorful and controversial of them. Her father was a wealthy banker and had been head of a Jewish congregation in Alexandria, Egypt before the family lived in Fostat.

Wuhsha remained unmarried for most of her life. A brief marriage to Arye ben Judah resulted in divorce in 1095. This divorce may have occurred after Wuhsha gave birth to a son, Abu Saad, who was not Arye's child. Since parts of the court records are missing, the facts concerning Wuhsha's love affair with Abu Saad's father, Hassun, are unclear. It is certain, however, that Wuhsha went to great lengths to establish the status and rights of her son under Jewish law. She wanted to make sure that he could marry a Jewish girl and remain in the Jewish community in spite of what she had done.

The Jews of Fostat disapproved of Wuhsha's activities. They even expelled her from a synagogue one Yom Kippur for her scandalous behavior with Hassun. Nevertheless, she remained an important figure in the community. She was rich and independent, and conducted successful business ventures until her death.

Geniza manuscripts reveal that Wuhsha also had a daughter, Ghazal, and a granddaughter.

Both of these women identified themselves as "the daughter of al Wuhsha." Both were active businesswomen, buying and repairing houses.

The most interesting of the documents concerning Wuhsha is her last will and testament. A wealthy woman when she died, and relatively young, Wuhsha left most of her estate to her young son. She was careful to describe exactly how she wanted him to be educated. She wrote:

> *The melamed (teacher), Rabbi Moses, shall be taken to (my son) and shall teach him the Bible and the prayer book to the degree it is appropriate that he should know them. The teacher shall be given a blanket and a sleeping carpet so that he can stay with him. He shall receive from the boy's estate every week five dirhams.*

Wuhsha also left money to charitable and religious organizations and to other relatives. Her daughter, already married, would have been provided for with a dowry. However, Wuhsha insisted that Hassun, Abu Saad's father "shall not get a penny."

A portion of Wuhsha's money was set aside for an elaborate funeral. Like other well-to-do women of her time, Wuhsha wore clothes of the most gorgeous colors and fabrics. Her dowry had included several expensive pieces of jewelry. Wuhsha's love of finery extended even to her death. She specified that her burial attire must be new, and requested that cantors walk behind her coffin chanting psalms.

Although Wuhsha was a rebel in her community, she teaches us that determined and talented women could achieve power and success even in places where women's lives were severely restricted.

An Unknown Mother

In an era when life was uncertain, and fortunes could be easily reversed, women were often determined to provide for their children at all costs. This was the case for one unnamed Egyptian Jewish woman who lived sometime before the thirteenth century. Seriously ill and far from her family, she wanted to insure not only that her daughter would be provided for, but that she would receive a Jewish education. In a touching letter, she wrote to her sister in Fostat:

My most urgent request to you, if God the Exalted indeed decrees my death, is to take care

of my little daughter and make efforts to give her an education, although I know well that I

am asking you for something unreasonable, as there is not enough money for maintenance,

let alone for education. However, she had a model in our mother, the saint.

This is only one example of a family where the tradition of educating women was a strong and continuing one. Such letters prove that despite Jewish restrictions on teaching women, some mothers arranged to have their daughters educated, even at great sacrifice.

A Captive Woman

The Crusades were a series of wars which began in the late eleventh century and continued for several hundred years. These wars were fought by European Christians who attempted to win Palestine from the ruling Muslims in order to maintain control of the holy places where they believed Jesus had once lived. During the fighting, many innocent people were killed or taken captive. It was common for soldiers to hold prisoners for ransom. The money they received from the prisoners' families helped finance the war.

Jews often suffered from such a practice, and Jewish communities regularly raised money to ransom captives. We know about one captive woman from a *Geniza* letter. Although the community had already redeemed her, she was now alone in Egypt with no money. Once again she appealed to the Jewish community:

I hereby inform the Holy Congregation — may God enhance its splendor — that I am a

woman who was taken captive in the land of Israel. I arrived here a week (ago) from

Sunbat, and I have no proper clothing, no blankets and no sleeping carpet. With me is

my little boy and I have no means of sustenance. I now beseech you, the Exalted, and

beseech the congregation — may you be blessed — to do what is proper to be done with

any wayfarer.

This brave woman, far from her home in Palestine, understood that only the Jewish community would help her. She is an example of hundreds — perhaps thousands — of Jewish women who suffered in this way during the Crusades. It is likely that many of them addressed letters to the entire congregation as well as to its communal leaders (the Exalted). Such letters were most probably read during the synagogue service.

Although the *Geniza* treasures do not reveal the fate of this woman and her child, it is reasonable to believe that the Jews of Fostat, following a long tradition of *tzedakah* (charity), helped her with money and contributions.

A sketch of the women's section of the Worms Synagogue.

Chapter 5

A Devotion to Learning

The first Crusade, which began in 1096, brought with it some disturbing events for the Jews, especially those living in Europe and the Middle East. Many Jews were taken as captives or killed in the course of war. In some European countries Jews were attacked by Crusaders and forced to convert to Christianity.

Such persecution sometimes made Jews more committed to their religion. From the late eleventh century, Jewish learning spread to all the major towns in Europe, and great scholars became famous throughout the Jewish world. In the academies (yeshivot) where these scholars taught, young Jewish men could come to study the law and the writings of the ancient sages.

A few women also became noted scholars. Although there were traditional limits on women's education, daughters of scholarly families sometimes became expert in Jewish law. An example of this is Rachel, one of the three daughters of Rashi.

Rashi, whose given name was Solomon ben Isaac, was a great Jewish scholar. He lived in Troyes, a town in northern France, from 1040 to 1105. During his lifetime Rashi wrote commentaries and explanations on most of the Bible and the Talmud. He also answered many questions about Jewish law for the Jews in his area.

Rachel, sometimes called by her French name, Belle-Assez, wrote advisory letters in her father's name when he was sick. One of Rashi's granddaughters, Hannah, was also knowledgeable in Jewish law and her opinions were valued.

Occasionally, learned women such as these were teachers in all-male academies. Though rare, there are documents that mention women teaching men in a few places in Europe and the Middle East from the eleventh to the sixteenth century. They usually taught from behind a screen, in the interests of modesty and to avoid distracting the male students. Modesty was a virtue traditionally expected of Jewish women.

WOMEN SCHOLARS IN THE LANDS OF THE MIDDLE EAST

The Daughter of the Levite

Although she is known simply as *Bat HaLevi* (the daughter of the Levite), the reputation of this young woman has lasted from the twelfth century until today. Her father, Samuel ben Ali the Levite, was the most prominent leader of the academy of Baghdad. He ruled over the Jewish communities of Baghdad and the surrounding areas for thirty years. Rabbi Samuel's yeshivah had long been an important center of Jewish learning and legal decisions. It reached the peak of its influence during his years of leadership and remained an important center until after his death in 1194.

Because he had no male children, Rabbi Samuel taught his daughter as if she were a son. She soon began to lecture students at the academy. Reportedly she taught from behind a screen or window so the men would not see her face.

A traveler of the time wrote that Samuel ben Ali's daughter was:

> . . . *expert in Scripture and Talmud. She gives instruction in Scripture to young men through a window. She herself is within the building, while the disciples are below outside and do not see her.*

There are only a few references to the details of Bat HaLevi's life, but there is little doubt that she actually existed. Rabbi Samuel's letters mention a beloved son-in-law who functioned as head of the academy and is assumed to have been her husband. Although the date of her death is unknown, Bat HaLevi is buried next to her father. Both graves were considered holy places to Sephardic Jews for many generations.

Lady Asenath Mizrahi

Lady Asenath Mizrahi, like Bat HaLevi, was an only child. She is believed to be the daughter of the rabbi and scholar Samuel Barazani, and she lived in the city of Mosul, in what is known today as Kurdistan.

Many Jews had found refuge in this area of Kurdistan after being chased from Baghdad in 1393. However, conditions in Mosul were also difficult and unstable. Little is known of the growth of the Jewish communities there before the sixteenth century, when Asenath Barazani lived.

As a young girl, Asenath received an excellent education in her father's academy. "I was raised on the knees of the greatest scholars," she would later write. Asenath was so well educated that she was able to assume all her father's teaching responsibilities. This freed him for his other duties as head of the Kurdistani Jewish community.

When Asenath married Jacob Mizrahi, her marriage contract stated that she would never have to do any housework. Instead, her time would be spent in study or teaching. This arrangement was an unusual one. It was widely accepted that a woman's only natural role and obligation was to tend the home and care for her husband and children.

During her marriage, Lady Mizrahi returned to teaching in the same yeshivah founded by her father and now run by her husband, Jacob. When Rabbi Jacob Mizrahi died, Lady Mizrahi made great efforts to maintain the school. She had to raise funds from the community and went into debt several times.

Lady Mizrahi described how the authorities sent agents to her home, who confiscated her property to satisfy the debts of the academy. In a desperate letter to the Jewish community of Amadiya, a nearby city, she wrote:

> *They caught me and hit me . . . they sent a judgment with people that took over my house and they sold everything; my clothes and my daughter's clothes. They even took the books that were before me!*

Lady Mizrahi pleaded with the Jewish community for money to help her continue her teaching. She wanted their support for the academy until her son, Samuel, was old enough to assist in the work. With courage and determination, she succeeded. Records indicate that Samuel Mizrahi later assumed the administrative and fund-raising duties of the school.

Nowhere in her letters does Lady Mizrahi refer to herself as anything but "your humble servant, the wife of Jacob Mizrahi." As a result, we are not sure that she was actually Rabbi Barazani's daughter Asenath, although many scholars believe that she was. "Lady" is a translation of the Hebrew word *marat*, a term of respect used for women. Even without a first name, however, this sixteenth-century woman is remarkable for her scholarship and perseverance; she is an inspiring example for our own time.

WOMEN SCHOLARS OF EUROPE

Dulcie of Worms

Dulcie of Worms was a scholar, a wife, a mother, and a working woman. She met a violent death at the hands of Christian intruders in 1196. They broke into her home expecting to find valuables. Her two young daughters, Bellet, aged 13, and Hannah, aged 6, were killed at the same time, and her husband and son were seriously wounded.

We know as much as we do about Dulcie because of these tragic events. Broken-hearted by his loss, her husband, Rabbi Eleazar ben Judah, wrote a moving poem about his wife and daughters. The opening lines of this poem, modeled after the biblical verses in the Book of Proverbs, read:

> *Who can find a woman of valor like my pietist wife, Mistress Dulcie?*
>
> *A woman of valor, her husband's crown, a daughter of aristocrats,*
>
> *A God-fearing woman, renowned for her good deeds;*
>
> *Her husband trusts her implicitly, she fed and clothed him in dignity.*

Dulcie was born into a prosperous and respected Jewish family in the Rhineland (German) town of Worms. She married Eleazar, descendent of a great scholarly family in Germany. The couple had two daughters and a son.

Pious and hardworking, Dulcie supported her family and also her husband's students, who boarded with them. She was a moneylender, and people deposited large sums of money with her. She lent out the money at interest and received a commission for her work.

Rabbi Eleazar's poem described in detail many of Dulcie's other activities. She taught women the prayers and songs associated with the synagogue service and was known for her sweet voice. Dulcie spun thread and sewed Torah scrolls, repaired torn books, and made wicks for the synagogue's candles. She also sewed clothes for the students, helped prepare brides for their weddings, and visited the sick. She did all this in addition to caring for her own family. This description gives us some idea of what daily life was like for Jewish women in Europe in the twelfth century.

In the same poem, Rabbi Eleazar wrote lovingly and proudly about the accomplishments of his daughters. Bellet learned prayers and melodies from her mother, helped around the house, and was accomplished in spinning, sewing, and embroidery. Even Hannah, only 6 years old, knew how to recite the Sh'ma prayer, and could spin, sew, and embroider.

The evidence from this poem suggests that Dulcie may have been one of the first women to formally lead synagogue prayer. Rabbi Eleazar affirmed that his wife spent many hours in the synagogue, "coming early and staying late." He also reported that she sang hymns and prayers and taught them to others. Such women later came to be called *firzogerins* or *zogerkes*, the Yiddish words for "foresayer" or "reciter."

By the twelfth century women were excluded from participation in the men's service in European synagogues. The *firzogerins* led the women in prayer in a separate section of the synagogue. Often they translated the prayers into the local language because women were rarely taught Hebrew.

Rabbi Eleazar described Dulcie as an active, energetic woman who was devoted to her family and her community. Along with her daughters, she became one of the many Jewish martyrs of the Middle Ages. However, it is not her tragic death, but the example of her life, which should be honored.

The women of Worms prayed in a separate room.

Lady Urania

From the gravestone of Lady Urania, a woman cantor, we can learn a great deal. She, too, lived in Worms, sometime during the thirteenth century, many years after Dulcie's death. In this Rhineland town, the women were said to have not merely a separate section, but a separate room in the synagogue, apart from the men.

Urania's father was a cantor and was referred to as the head of the synagogue singers. She herself was a *firzogerin* in the women's synagogue. Her tombstone reads:

> *This headstone commemorates the eminent and excellent Lady Urania, the daughter of Rabbi Abraham, who was the chief of the synagogue singers.*

His prayer for his people rose up unto glory. And as to her, she, too, with sweet tunefulness,

officiated before the female worshipers to whom she sang the hymnal portions. In devout service,

her memory shall be preserved.

Miriam Shapira-Luria

Miriam Shapira-Luria was a teacher of Talmud in the Jewish academy in Padua, Italy. According to many reports, she taught from behind a latticed screen so the male students would not be distracted by her beauty.

Miriam was the daughter of Solomon Shapira (or Spira), founder of the Shapira-Luria family. She lived in Italy in the first half of the fourteenth century and was already teaching in Padua in 1350. Born into a learned family, Miriam lived at the beginning of an exciting era referred to as the Renaissance, or rebirth.

The Renaissance spanned approximately two and a half centuries, from the early 1300s to the end of the 1500s. During this time, respect for learning among Jews and gentiles was at its height. Padua boasted its own university where both Jewish and Christian scholars lectured to a growing body of students.

Miriam, probably an only child, married Yohanan ben Luria, also a noted scholar. Although there is no clear record of their children, descendants of Miriam and Yohanan made their marks in the Jewish world. The Shapira-Luria family was known and respected throughout France, Italy, and Germany for several hundred years after Miriam lived and taught.

Miriam Shapira-Luria's reputation as a learned woman has persisted through the centuries. Although hidden behind legends and lattices, her name stands out as an early example of women's scholarship.

Rebecca Tiktiner

Rebecca Tiktiner, daughter of Rabbi Meir Tiktiner, is a voice that comes down to us from the sixteenth century. Her last name suggests that she lived in the Polish town of Tiktin. Other sources say that Rebecca lived in Prague.

Little is known about Rebecca's personal life. There is no record of her marriage, although it was customary for Jewish women to be married at a young age.

Rebecca is known only by her writings. These include a book called *Meneket Rivkah (Rebecca's Nursemaid)*, and "Song for Simhat Torah," a long prayer to be recited on Simhat

Torah. Rebecca also translated a well-known ethical work from the twelfth century called *Duties of the Heart*. Tiktiner is considered to be the first woman to have written and published works in Judeo-German, the language that evolved into Yiddish.

Two editions of *Meneket Rivkah* were printed after Rebecca's death in 1550. In the introduction to the 1618 version, Rebecca Tiktiner is referred to by the printer as "a *rebbetzin* preacher." This statement probably meant that she, like Dulcie before her, was the wife of a rabbi and a *firzogerin* in the women's section of the synagogue.

Rebecca's book may even have been compiled from her lectures to the women. It showed a wide knowledge of Jewish literature, including moral teachings, selections from the Talmud and Mishnah, poetry, and Jewish legends.

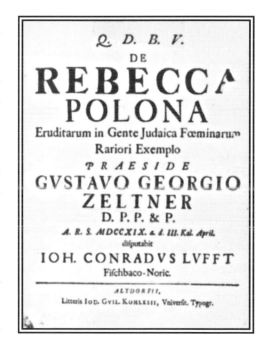

A large section of the book gave advice to mothers about raising children. Rebecca taught mothers how to nurse and bathe their babies. She also guided women on education. The minds of young children, she said, are like clean slates. Mothers have the chance to write on those slates, and they should not waste the opportunity.

Rebecca suggested that mothers should study Torah together with their children and carefully teach them right and wrong. They were also urged to teach their children "the holy language." This implied that women as well as men should know Hebrew. It must have been surprising for women to read such advice from Rebecca's book since they were rarely taught Hebrew or Torah.

The title page of a book written about Rebecca Tiktiner by a Christian scholar in 1719.

In 1719, one hundred and sixty-nine years after Rebecca Tiktiner's death, Gustav George Zeltner, a Christian clergyman, published a book about her. Zeltner was impressed with Rebecca's broad knowledge. He referred to her as "the Polish Rebecca, a rather rare example of learned women in the Jewish nation." Since the eighteenth century, Rebecca Tiktiner has been forgotten by history. However, her accomplishments and her support for women's education identify her as one of the earliest Jewish feminists.

מעשה ידי הבחורה יראת יְיָ
ומשכלת מרת אילי מִבַּת בַּת
איש חיל רב פְעָלִים כּמ מנחם
הלוי משולמם יְצֹו ‏ ‏ ‏

ויהי השלמתו ברביעִי בשבת יוּם
ראש השנה לשנות טו לחדש
שלום בְרכָה טֹובה בשנת
למען תַּלְמֹד ליראה
את יְיָ

Part of a manuscript of daily prayers copied by an Italian Jewish woman.

Chapter 6

The Fruit of Their Hands

Before the industrial revolution, when production moved into factories, most work was done at home in family workshops. This made it relatively easy for women and girls to be trained in the family occupation. The wife and mother of the family was often responsible for much of the production. Because it was happening at home, this work was not separated from the other household chores. The result was that many women were skilled in crafts, having learned their professions either from their parents or, later, from their husbands.

One of the oldest and most honored professions among Jews was that of scribe. The scribe had to be able to read and write. Having good handwriting and a steady hand were also important. In addition to writing, most scribes made their own ink and pens and prepared the parchment themselves. They usually worked at writing tables, in workshops in their own homes.

In families where the father earned his living as a scribe, the entire family often helped him with this work. Such was the case with the family of the scribe Banayah.

Miriam the Scribe

Records show that in the fifteenth century a woman named Miriam lived in the remote desert land of Yemen. Miriam was the daughter of Banayah, head of the most famous family of scribes in Yemen. She had two brothers, Joseph and David; all three siblings worked with their father. They copied Torah scrolls, Haftarot (Books of the Prophets), and prayer books, all in Hebrew. Together, the family produced a total of approximately 400 volumes.

Women rarely knew how to read and write in fifteenth century Yemen. It was even more uncommon for women to be scribes. In the capital city of San'a where she lived with her family, Miriam was an exception.

After her marriage, Miriam continued working with her father. At the end of a Torah she copied, she wrote: "Do not condemn me for any errors that you may find, for I am a nursing woman." She signed her note "Miriam, the daughter of Banayah the scribe."

Paula Dei Mansi

A few other women have left such signatures in books that they copied. One of them was Paula, the daughter of Abraham Anau, and a member of a distinguished family of Jewish scribes in Rome.

The name Anau has been traced back to ancient Judea. It means modest or meek and was translated into Italian in many different ways. Members of this family were known as De Mansi, Piatelli, Pietosa, or Umani. All were part of the same large family, which traced their roots back to Yehiel ben Abraham. This noted Jewish scholar lived in Rome where he headed the yeshivah and was famous for his poetry. He died late in the eleventh century.

Paula, the daughter of Abraham ben Joab, was Yehiel's great granddaughter. She first married Solomon de Rossi, with whom she had three sons, Immanuel, Yekutiel, and Solomon. Paula named her youngest boy, born in 1285 after her husband's death, for his father. There were no children from a second marriage to Yehiel ben Solomon de Mansi (probably a distant cousin).

In 1288, Paula translated her father's commentary on the prophets from Hebrew into Italian, adding her own observations. In the front of the manuscript, she signed her name and included her full family tree. The inscription reads: "This book, the commentary on the Prophets, was written by the hand of Paula, daughter of Rabbi Abraham the Scribe, son of Rabbi Joab, from the son of his son, of Rabbi Yehiel, father of Rabbenu Nathan . . . ."

Two other books, both the products of Paula's pen, are preserved in European libraries. A prayer book with explanations was dedicated to her son, then eight years old. In it she wrote: "This was completed . . . in the year 1293 by the hands of Paula, the daughter of Rabbi Abraham the Scribe, the son of Joab, and I wrote it in the name of my son Solomon, the son of my honored teacher, Rabbi Solomon" (her first husband). She added: "May He Who has made me worthy to write this, make me worthy to see (my son) great in Torah, in wisdom, and in fear of God."

Also in 1293, Paula copied a collection of laws for another relative, Menahem ben Benjamin the Zaddik. Again she inscribed a lengthy passage at the beginning of the work. This inscription acknowledged that "my dear relative came to me and entreated, begged, and compelled me to write this holy book for him . . . With the help of God I made a great effort in this work and finished it . . . on Wednesday, the second day of the first month *(Tishrei)* in the year of 1293 . . . ."

The Dei Mansi/Anau family continued to produce many generations of scholars. Although the official family tree records only the names of the male members, Paula was part of a distinguished line of copyists and maintained the high standard established by her ancestors.

Frommet Arwyller

Frommet Arwyller (or Ahrweiler) is another Jewish woman who used her skill with a pen as a gift of love. Little is known of her origins. Her name suggests that either she or her father originated in the town of Ahrweiler, in Germany. Frommet copied a short version of a Jewish code of laws known as *Kizzur Mordecai*. In it she wrote: "This copy has been executed by Frommet, daughter of Arwyller, for her husband, Samuel ben Moses, 1454." This rare work is presently preserved in the National Library of France, in Paris.

WOMEN PRINTERS

Johannes Gutenberg produced the first printed edition of the Bible on a printing press, in 1455. Gutenberg himself was not a Jew, but his invention was quickly adopted by the Jewish community. By the end of the fifteenth century, many Jewish presses functioned throughout Europe, the Middle East, and North Africa. Because printing continued to be done mainly in home workshops, women played a large part in producing books.

One of the earliest known Jewish woman printers was Estellina Conat, wife of Abraham Conat of Mantua, Italy. The Conats were active typesetters and printers from 1476 to 1480, and Estellina is known to have set the type for at least one of the books which their workshop produced.

Many other women participated in printing as part of family businesses, often maintaining a workshop alone after the death of a husband. Large families of printers can sometimes be traced over several generations.

A man and a woman working together at an early printing press.

Ella bat Moses

Children often worked next to their parents, helping with all kinds of jobs in a family business. Although these children usually remained anonymous, some printed pages, left by a few young girls, give us a rare glimpse into the lives and work of one family of printers.

Ella, daughter of the printer Moses ben Abraham, lived with her family in Dessau, Germany. In 1696 she set the type for a Hebrew prayer book with a Yiddish translation. This suggests that she could read and write in both Hebrew and Yiddish. At the bottom of one page, she proudly acknowledges her work, done "by my own hand." She describes herself as "an only daughter among six children" and asks to be excused from any printer's errors since she is only nine years old.

A few other books printed by Ella bear similar inscriptions. Ella describes one of them as "a beautiful new book of prayers, never before printed in translation." She credits a "pious Jewish woman" who donated money to have the prayers translated. Usually translations into the local language were made so that women, as well as uneducated men who could not read Hebrew, would understand the prayers.

Ella also worked for a while in her brother's printshop in Frankfurt. During her stay there, she helped typeset the Frankfurt edition of the Talmud, the most important publication to come out of this major center of Hebrew printing.

Gela bat Moses

Gela was Ella's younger sister, born after 1696. When the family moved to the town of Halle, she, too, worked in the family printing business. From the short poem she composed at the end of a collection of prayers, we know a little more about the Ben Abraham family. Gela and Ella's mother, who had a total of ten children, was herself the daughter of a rabbi. Their father, Moses ben Abraham, had converted to Judaism in Amsterdam and then moved to Germany.

Gela's Yiddish poem, part of which is printed below, is dated 1713.

> *Of this beautiful prayer book from beginning to end,*
>
> *I set all the letters in type with my own hands.*
>
> *I, Gela, the daughter of Moses the printer, and whose mother*
>
> *was Freide, the daughter of R. Israel Katz, may his memory be*
>
> *for a blessing. She bore me among ten children:*
>
> *I am a maiden still somewhat under twelve years.*
>
> *It is not unusual that I must work;*
>
> *The tender and delicate daughter of Israel has been in*

exile for a long time.

One year passes and another comes

And we have not yet heard of any redemption . . .

Rebecca, Daughter of Israel the Printer

Ella's and Gela's brother, Israel, set up his own print shop in the nearby town of Frankfurt. For a while, Ella helped him there. After he married, his own daughter, Rebecca, worked with him. Like her aunts, she began working when she was very young, and she, too, left her mark in the books for which she set the type.

At the end of the first part of a prayer book she wrote:

I did this with my own hands, Rebecca, daughter of Israel, the owner of the printing press.

Dear reader, if you find any mistakes, please excuse them, for I am only a child.

WOMEN PUBLISHERS

Many other women were committed to the spread of learning through the printed word. Although not working scribes or printers themselves, they supervised, or donated money for, the printing of books.

Among these patrons was Reyna Nasi of Turkey, daughter of the famous Dona Gracia Nasi (see Chapter 8). She ran her own press between 1578 and 1600. An early imprint in Reyna Nasi's books read: "Printed in the Palace of the Honored Woman, Reyna Nasi, widow of the Duke Don Joseph Nasi, at Belvedere which is near Constantinople, under the rule of Sultan Murad."

Edel, daughter of Joshua Menahem Mendel of Prague was another woman publisher whose generosity is recorded. She was acknowledged as the benefactor of one book of prayers, printed in 1655. The inscription reads: "To the memory of the wise woman, the preacher, the great and pious Lady Edel . . . who took the money from her own pocket to benefit the many and brought these prayers to be printed."

These women — scribes, typesetters, and patrons of publishing — used the production of religious books as an expression of their commitment to God. Through the routine tasks of writing, translating and printing, they passed on their spirituality and devotion to the Jewish people.

Typical Jewish Renaissance women from Ferrara, Italy.

Chapter 7

Italian Poets and Singers

The discovery of printing helped to spread new ideas throughout Europe. In Italy especially, where the Renaissance began in the early 1300s, painting, music, dance, and poetry flourished. Historians have described the years between 1450 and 1650 as a time of cultural reawakening. Non-religious art forms developed, especially in northern Italy. Many Jews who were expelled from Spain in 1492 found a haven in the cultured and active Jewish communities of Italy.

By the early 1500s, large numbers of *Sephardim* had expanded the Italian-Jewish population. A Spanish translation of the Hebrew Bible was printed in Ferrara, Italy by mid-century, and congregations of Sephardic Jews appeared throughout the peninsula. By the mid-1550s, though, the Renaissance had reached its peak and was beginning to fade.

Changes were taking place in Italy that affected the creative climate. In 1516, for the first time, Jews were forced to live in one particular section of the city of Venice. This Jewish area was originally called a ghetto because it was near an iron foundry (*geto* or *ghetto* in Italian). As the century advanced, one Italian city after another separated their Jews into ghettos.

Despite this new policy of segregation, Jews continued to participate as fully as possible in the cultural life of their communities. There were Jewish scholars, doctors, entertainers, musicians, playwrights, and poets in all the Italian cities. Some of these individuals were women.

Madame Europa

One Jewish woman who gained fame as a performer was from the De Rossi family of Mantua, Italy. Her given name is not known. Her stage name, Madame Europa, was taken from a part she played in a musical production by the composer Monteverdi. This production was part of the wedding celebration for the son of the Duke of Mantua and the Princess of Savoy in 1608.

Madame Europa was highly praised for her performance. It was said that she understood music to perfection and "sang to the great pleasure . . . of the audience, her voice being so delicate and sweet . . . bringing tears to their eyes." Through this role Madame Europa first became famous as a singer and entertainer.

Solomon De Rossi, Madame Europa's brother, was a leading performer and composer. He worked as a court musician for the Dukes of Mantua. Solomon wrote music, played the viola, and sang. Madame Europa also performed regularly at the royal court.

Madame Europa married David ben Elisha, a scholar who wrote many books. Two of their sons, Angelo (Mordecai) and Benaiuto (Azariah), inherited their mother's talents and became court musicians. A third son, Anselmo (Asher), was a leader of the Jewish community. He, too, sometimes participated in the elaborate performances produced at the royal court.

Despite the growing restrictions faced by Jews in Italy, and the traditional limits placed on women, Madame Europa was a talented musician who lived life in the spotlight.

Devorah Ascarelli

Devorah Ascarelli of Rome was both a scholar and a poet. Fluent in Hebrew, she translated important religious books and poetry into Italian. She also wrote original poems. Devorah was the first Jewish woman to have her work published in the Italian language.

Joseph Ascarelli, Devorah's husband, was a successful merchant and an active member of the Catalan synagogue in Rome. The Catalan synagogue was first organized by Sephardic Jews coming from the province of Catalonia in Spain. For some time Joseph Ascarelli served as its president. Devorah, like Dulcie of Worms and Rebecca Tiktiner, was probably a teacher and leader in the women's section of that synagogue. Many of her Italian translations were written in the Hebrew alphabet. This suggests that they may have been prepared especially for the women of her congregation.

Devorah Ascarelli's poetry was first published in 1602 in Venice. It was forgotten for many centuries and then reissued by a descendent of the Ascarelli family in 1925. Devorah Ascarelli is one of the few Italian Jewish women scholars known to us today.

Devorah Ascarelli, Italian scholar and poet.

Sara Coppio Sullam

Sara was born to Rebecca and Simon Coppio in the ghetto of Venice in 1592. By this time, the Renaissance was beginning to decline, but Jews and Christians still mingled and exchanged ideas.

As the only child in a prosperous and well-known Venetian Jewish family, Sara received a fine education. By the time she was fifteen, she could read five languages: Latin, Greek, Spanish, Hebrew, and Italian.

Sara began writing poetry at a very early age and continued after her marriage to Jacob Sullam in 1614. Her work was much admired by non-Jews as well as Jews. In the Venetian ghetto, her home was a popular literary salon, attracting Jews and Christians alike. She was a patron of poets and writers, supporting them with money in return for lessons and poems.

Sara was active and well-known in the world of art and literature. She shared her ideas with Christian thinkers. Among them was Anseldo Cena, a distinguished Italian nobleman from Genoa. Like Sara, he was a poet and scholar.

Sara first began corresponding with him just a few years after her marriage, when she wrote to praise one of his poems. From these beginnings a friendship developed. Although the two poets never met, they exchanged more than fifty letters and poems. In most of them, Anseldo Cena tried to convince Sara to become a Christian. He could not imagine that such a talented and intelligent woman would want to continue being a Jew. In one of his poems, he described her as "still in the darkness of Hebraic rites." Despite Cena's best attempts, however, Sara remained true to her religion and her people.

As she grew older, many of Sara's Christian admirers began to resent her because of her refusal to convert to Christianity. One bishop falsely accused her of denying the immortality of the soul. This implied that she did not believe in life after death.

This accusation put Sara Coppio Sullam in great danger. In most of the western world, in the twentieth century, a charge that someone is not religious, or does not believe in the human soul, is not life-threatening. In 1621, however, the situation was different. The Catholic Church was strong and demanded that all people think alike in matters of religion. Jews, too, were expected to accept certain basic ideas about God and human beings. If they did not, they might be arrested, imprisoned, and even killed.

Understanding her situation, Sara hurried to deny the charge. She wrote a pamphlet insisting that she did believe in the soul's immortality. The pamphlet was dedicated to her father, who had died when Sara was fifteen years old. As she explained, the work "could not properly be dedicated to anybody else." By inscribing it to someone already dead, she believed she was helping to prove that she did indeed have faith in a life after death.

Although Sara was not arrested for her beliefs, dangerous reports about her lack of faith continued. Her writing shows how saddened and angry she was by these rumors. In one sonnet she asks God, "[Who knows] my inmost hope and thought," to silence the "venom" of the "lying tongue's deceit" and protect her from "spiteful slanderers."

Sara Coppio Sullam only lived to the age of fifty. She died of a fever in 1641. No record of any of her descendants has been found, and she may never have had any children. During her lifetime, she became known as a generous woman who helped many people in need. This is reflected on her tombstone, which reads in part: "Lady Sara . . . Wise among wives, the support of derelicts. The wretched found in her a companion and friend."

Once described as "a great beauty, with blond hair and gentle glance," Sara was most remembered for other traits. She was generous and charming, educated and talented — a woman devoted to her people and courageous in the face of danger.

In the sixteenth and seventeenth centuries the Italian peninsula was divided into several independent states.

Chapter 8

Politics and Power

Jews played a major role in international trade in Europe during the fifteenth and sixteenth centuries. Some Sephardic women were among the most enterprising Jews to run large trading businesses. Others were successful bankers in the service of the nobility. Many also made contributions to medicine and the arts.

Women traders usually began as partners with their husbands. They worked in every aspect of commerce, from running small shops in local markets, to shipping, banking, and wholesale trade.

A few women became outstanding and successful business leaders, usually after their husbands died. As heads of important commercial establishments, they were then in a position to try to influence political decisions concerning Jews.

Benvenida Abrabanel

Benvenida was born into the rich and powerful Abrabanel family. The Abrabanels originated in Spain. They were close to the Spanish royal family and were active in the world of finance. When all Jews were expelled from the country in 1492, the Abrabanels left Spain

One branch, consisting of the brothers Isaac, Jacob, and Joseph, settled in Naples, Italy. They were rich and well-respected. Jacob Abrabanel became head of the Jewish community of Naples. Benvenida was his daughter.

Benvenida received a fine education in both Jewish and secular subjects. Even among a family of scholars, she was admired for her learning. When she was old enough, a marriage was arranged with her cousin Samuel, one of Isaac's sons.

Isaac, a successful banker in Italy, was also a student of Jewish law. Samuel had inherited his father's skill in finance and became advisor to the King of Naples. This relationship brought the couple close to the royal court where Benvenida's knowledge and talents did not go unnoticed.

When the Spanish Viceroy of Naples needed a teacher for his young daughter, Eleonora, he chose Benvenida Abrabanel. Benvenida taught Eleonora throughout her youth and remained her friend and confidant after she grew up and married.

Through this relationship, Benvenida Abrabanel maintained a great deal of influence in the politics of Naples. She did not hesitate to use either her connections or her money in the service of her people.

In 1532 the priests of the Inquisition were very active in all the cities of Italy. In their attempt to "purify" the Catholic religion of outside influences, a group of these priests petitioned the king of Naples. They wanted him to drive out the remaining Jews from southern Italy. With some exceptions for the richest Jews, the king granted the petition.

Benvenida appealed to her friend, Eleonora, now Duchess of Tuscany, for help in stopping the expulsion. Samuel Abrabanel also attempted to exert influence by bribing the authorities. However, the order was only postponed for seven years. In 1540 the Abrabanels, along with all the remaining Jews, had to leave Naples.

Such a powerful and influential family would not be homeless for long. They quickly accepted an invitation offered by the Duke of Ferrara and settled in that northern Italian city. Here Samuel and Benvenida's banking business prospered.

When Samuel died in 1547, Benvenida took over. Through the influence of Duchess Eleonora, she was granted important commercial privileges in Tuscany, an area bordering Ferrara. Her business flourished.

Benvenida was also well known for her charity and piety. She personally ransomed one thousand Jewish captives and donated large sums to Jewish settlements in Palestine.

When Benvenida Abrabanel died in 1560, she was described by a contemporary as "noble and high-spirited." He called her "a pattern of chastity, of piety, of prudence and of worth."

Dona Gracia Nasi

Gracia Nasi is considered one of the greatest women in the history of the Jewish people. This is so even though she was born in Portugal, into a *Marrano* family. Being a *Marrano* meant that she had to hide her Jewish beliefs and act like an observant Catholic. Portuguese Jews had been pretending to be Christians even before 1497, when all Jews were expelled from Portugal.

Gracia was born in the year 1510. Her Portuguese name was Beatrice de Luna and she was known by that name throughout her early life. Her family was wealthy, and her fortune increased when she married Francisco Mendes at the age of eighteen. Francisco was also a *Marrano* and was a successful banker and broker. The couple had one daughter, Brianda, later known as Reyna.

Reyna was a young child when her father died. Her mother, Beatrice, had inherited a vast

A bronze medal of Dona Gracia Nasi

fortune and a thriving business. In spite of her wealth, life was not easy. As the Inquisition became increasingly active in Portugal, *Marranos* were tracked down, tortured, and killed. Beatrice realized that she would have to leave her home.

At the age of twenty-six, with a young child to care for, Beatrice made an important decision. In 1537, she journeyed to Antwerp, capital of Flanders. She was accompanied by her daughter, her sister, and a nephew Joseph, then only thirteen years old.

In Antwerp, Beatrice began working with Diogo, her late husband's brother and partner. Together, they expanded their trading and banking business. During those years, she also became active in helping *Marranos* to escape Portugal and the Inquisition.

The family remained in Flanders until Diogo died. When a Catholic nobleman wanted to marry Reyna, the proposal created a serious problem. Because Antwerp was part of the Spanish Empire at that time, Beatrice was still pretending to be a Christian. However, determined that her daughter would marry a Jew, she tried to delay the offer of marriage. Unaware that Reyna and her family were Jewish, no one could understand why they would refuse such a prestigious match.

Beatrice realized that she would not be able to resist this pressure without revealing her true identity. She made another difficult decision. One morning, towards the end of 1544, Beatrice's palace in Antwerp was found abandoned. Taking only her jewels and personal belongings, she had fled with Reyna into Italy.

The family's first stop was Venice and then Ferrara, Italy. There Beatrice, safe from the dangers of the Inquisition, at last openly admitted her Judaism. She adopted the translation of her Hebrew name, *Hannah* (Grace). From that time onward, she was known as Dona Gracia Nasi. The name *Nasi* was her original family name and means prince. *Dona* is the Spanish-Portuguese title for lady.

From Italy, Dona Gracia continued her work supervising her vast banking and shipping empire and aiding other *Marranos* fleeing from Portugal. She also gave money for the first translation of the Hebrew Bible into Spanish. Finally, Gracia and Reyna settled in Constantinople, capital of the Ottoman (Turkish) Empire and a haven for Jews in the sixteenth century.

Joseph, Gracia's nephew, also embraced Judaism at this time. He and Reyna were married in 1554. Joseph became a close friend of the sultan of Turkey who appointed him Duke of Naxos in 1566. Naxos is a small island off the coast of Greece that was then under Turkish rule.

Gracia's business prospered in Turkey. She was one of the largest importers of cloth into Europe. Her ships traded in spices, grain, wool, and textiles from the East. She continued to administer her many enterprises and was a leader of the Jewish business community.

During the period from 1556 to 1557, a tragic event occurred in the seaport of Ancona, Italy, that would test Gracia's leadership abilities. The Inquisition had arrested twenty-five *Marrano* merchants trading and living in Ancona and had them burned at the stake. The Jewish community was horrified but unsure whether to take action.

Dona Gracia had a plan. She wanted all Jewish merchants to boycott the port of Ancona. That would mean no trade in and out of that city by Jewish or *Marrano* merchants, and no Jewish ships entering or leaving the port. Ancona would be brought to its knees and other cities would be warned not to persecute Jews.

This first economic boycott in recorded history was not successful. Too many people disagreed with Gracia's plan. They thought it was too dangerous for the Jews to force a change in Church policy for economic reasons. Dona Gracia was bitterly disappointed by the failure. She felt that Jews needed to actively fight persecution.

By the time she was in her fifties, Gracia had achieved fame and riches beyond imagination. She lived in a palace with many servants and attendants and dressed like a noblewoman. She extended her charity throughout the community and fed eighty poor people in her house daily. She also became a great patron of scholars, schools, and synagogues.

Dona Gracia Nasi was respected and loved by Jews and admired by the Turkish nobility. Through her wealth and her friends in high places, Gracia was able to protect members of her family. By a private arrangement with the sultan, she set up a yeshivah and a settlement for Jews in Palestine, then part of the Turkish Empire.

After her death in 1568, one man called her "the heart of her people." Another spoke of her as "the crown of glory of goodly women."

Gracia's daughter Reyna followed the example set by her mother. She continued to work on behalf of the Jewish community of Constantinople. Reyna Nasi is best known for her support of Jewish publications. Books from several Turkish presses were dedicated to her. Like Dona Gracia, she was a respected and honored lady. She died in 1598, thirty years after her mother.

Esther Kiera Handali

Esther Handali was a working woman — a woman who obtained wealth and influence without benefit of inheritance. Born early in the sixteenth century, she married Elijah Handali. The couple lived in Turkey and earned their livelihood by selling trinkets and jewelry to the sultan's harem in Constantinople. From these humble beginnings, Esther worked her way to power and influence.

Through her activities as a peddler, Esther first met the women of the sultan's harem. She was soon given an exemption from taxes by Sultan Suleiman as a reward for services to his mother. After her husband's death, Esther Handali took on increasing responsibilities for the royal harem and was known as Esther Kiera.

The word *kiera* designated a specific job in the sultan's palace. The *kiera* bought and sold clothing, cosmetics, and jewelry for the women of the harem. She might also run errands, carry messages, and perform other useful tasks.

These services were necessary because, by custom, Muslim women were forbidden to go out. They could not even be seen by men other than those in their immediate families. Therefore, a go-between was needed — someone who could be trusted and would be able to move freely between the harem and the streets. This position was often held by Jewish women. They became links between the royal harem and the outside world.

In her position as *kiera*, Esther Handali gradually earned the confidence of Safieh, the favorite wife of Sultan Murad III. Through Safieh's influence, Esther Kiera gained her own powerful status. She carried out diplomatic missions for the sultana in Venice, acting either as a translator or as a spy for the Turkish Empire. As a reward, she was granted the right to start her own lottery in the Venetian Republic. In connection with this business venture, orders were issued on her behalf by the sultan and by Venetian officials.

During this decade, from 1580 to 1590, Esther's wealth and privileges were at their height. Diplomatic observers considered her to be one of the most influential persons at court. She intervened in many court appointments and freely accepted gifts and bribes in return for her favors.

At the same time, Esther also gained a reputation for charity and good works. When anti-Jewish riots occurred, she often helped Jewish merchants whose shops were looted by Muslims. She fed the poor in her home, supported scholars, and financed the printing of Jewish books. When Sultan Murad III threatened to destroy the Jewish community, Esther Kiera prevented the decree from being enforced.

By 1595, Sultan Murad was dead. He left behind a troubled empire, filled with unrest and civil war. His son and successor, Muhammed III, wanted to assert his dominance over his influential mother Safieh and establish his own authority.

Over the years, Esther had learned the skills of using power and made many enemies. The sultan's mother, Safieh, now an old woman, was no longer able to intervene in her friend's behalf. Without royal protection Esther quickly lost her privileged position.

In 1600, Esther Kiera was past eighty years old and still trying to exercise political power. She attempted once more to influence the affairs of the court, replacing one official with another of her own choosing. Furious at this treachery, allies of the deposed official dragged Esther from the palace and brutally stabbed her. At least one of her sons was also executed at the same time. Her enormous fortune was confiscated by the sultan.

Thus ended the life of this complicated and powerful woman. During her lifetime Esther Kiera was both greedy and charitable, foolish and shrewd. At times her behavior was in conflict with Jewish standards. However, she used her wealth and influence on behalf of the Jewish people in Turkey.

The boundaries of European countries were continually changing in the seventeenth century. Arrows show the mail route between Prague and Vienna.

Chapter 9

Lost and Found: The Voices of Daily Life

By the end of the fifteenth century, for political, economic, or religious reasons, the Jews had been expelled from most of western Europe. Jews from England and France resettled in the newly developing towns of eastern Germany (*Ashkenaz* in Hebrew). Large numbers of Ashkenazim emigrated even further south and east, into the Austro-Hungarian Empire, Poland, and Bohemia. With this movement of populations, the traditional centers of Jewish learning shifted eastward, enriching the small Jewish communities already there.

By 1600, Prague, the capital of Bohemia (now the Czech Republic), included a major Jewish community. Jews had a long history of persecution in this city and had to live within a ghetto. However, from 1576 to 1611 they prospered under the rule of King Rudolph II. King Mathias, his successor, continued Rudolph's pro-Jewish policies until his death in 1619.

One year before Mathias' death, a major war broke out that would last for thirty years. It involved almost all the countries and rulers of central and eastern Europe. One of its causes was a conflict between Catholics and Protestants. Each king, duke, and local lord wanted his own territory to be unified under his religion. Many disagreements resulted.

This war, called the Thirty Years War, led to many changes of borders and rulers. It also affected the lives of individual Jews and Christians. The fighting made travel unsafe for everyone. Prices rose and goods were in short supply. Anti-Jewish riots by dissatisfied citizens created an added danger for Jews, who were concentrated in ghettos.

We can learn some of the details of this difficult period from a series of personal letters. One was written by a woman named Sarel Gutman.

Sarel Gutman

In 1619, Sarel Gutman was a mature woman with a married daughter. Sarel and her husband, Loeb, made a living as merchants. Although they lived in Prague, Loeb often traveled to Vienna and other towns in Austria to buy and sell merchandise.

To keep in touch with each other, the couple organized a private mail service between Prague and Vienna. Long before governments provided such services, Sarel and Loeb paid messengers to carry mail for them and their neighbors. Several times a week, letters and packages were transported 160 miles back and forth between the two cities. Sarel collected a fee for the service from people posting mail in Prague, while Loeb was responsible for letters sent from Vienna.

On Friday, November 22, 1619, just before the Sabbath began, Sarel sent a long letter to her husband. It went into a large sack with other letters and packages. Before dark on that Friday evening, the Gutman's messenger had already left for Vienna. But the mail he carried would never be delivered.

Austrian soldiers, patrolling the border that night, apprehended the messenger. Thinking his bundle might contain some important communication, they confiscated it. When the soldiers realized that the bag held no information of value for the war, they tossed Sarel's letter, along with many others, into a storeroom.

The stack of mail was shoved into a corner and forgotten by everyone. It remained there long after the war ended. Three hundred years later, it was rediscovered, and Sarel added a small piece to Jewish history.

In her letter, Sarel Gutman reported to her husband that a new king and queen had just been crowned in Prague: Frederick I and his wife Elizabeth of England. Beyond these bare facts, Sarel also wrote of the dangers of her life in the ghetto:

I have much to write you about horrible things, but I cannot write about the affliction we had to

endure here when riots almost occurred in our streets. It was like at the destruction of the Temple

. . . Now we have been saved from this peril, we have certainly profited by the merits of our

ancestors.

A Jewish woman alone during wartime faced many dangers and threats. Soldiers or rioting citizens might rape or kill her. She might die for lack of food and medical supplies or be seized and held for ransom. If she had no money to pay, she would almost certainly be killed. Sarel spoke about these dangers in the letter:

I have not saved a penny for my own needs, if, God forbid, my life were to be endangered.

Nowadays nobody is ready to lend anything to other people . . . When I needed something for a

living, I was obliged to offer double pledges and to pay high interest. What could I do? . . . As saying goes: Need breaks iron . . . You must eat, domestics must eat. You may be as careful as you like, you must have money anyhow.

In the face of war and deprivation, Sarel, like so many other strong women, continued to maintain her household alone. She managed to borrow money to feed herself and the servants who were dependent on her. Rather than calling for her husband to return and help her, Sarel wrote:

Believe me, therefore, my head tells me not to wish you now here. I think you are yourself prudent enough for this . . . If I only hear where you are in the world, if I only hear about you and I have a letter from you every week and know that you have a good job. For here one cannot do anything nowadays, until the Lord, be He praised, will change it soon for the better.

Sarel didn't ask for assistance from her husband; she only wanted to be sure Loeb was healthy and safe, since she had not heard from him for seven weeks. "Honestly," she wrote, "I do not know how I live in my great distress."

Historians will probably never discover what happened to Sarel and Loeb. In the chaos of the Thirty Years War they may have perished along with many other Jews and Christians. However, Sarel's words reveal a self-reliance and quiet heroism in difficult times. Her unique character traits and her concern for her loved ones surely provided an example for her own daughter and for continuing generations.

Gluckel of Hameln

Gluckel Pinkerle was one of many children. She was born in 1646, and lived in Hamburg, Germany with her family. In 1648, when Gluckel was only two years old, all the Jews were expelled from that city.

This expulsion was one of many changes that occurred in Europe. A major shift of populations was part of the peace settlement of 1648 between Protestants and Catholics, which ended the Thirty Years War. Jews, caught in this power struggle, often suffered from religious and economic policies over which they had no control.

Gluckel and her family moved to nearby Altona, then under Danish rule. They lived peacefully in Altona until 1657, when war broke out once more, this time between Denmark and

Sweden. When Altona was attacked by the Swedes, the Jews fled back to Hamburg where they were again granted permission to live.

Shortly after this event, in her twelfth year, Gluckel was betrothed to a young boy, Hayyim. At the age of fourteen, she was married. In the seventeenth century it was still accepted practice for young women to be married in their early teens. Often, the young bride did not know the groom at all. Gluckel never questioned this arrangement and went to live with her husband's family in the small town of Hameln.

Writing about her life many years later, she recalled:

> *And there I was — a carefree child whisked in the flush of youth from parents, friends, and everyone I knew, from a city like Hamburg plump into a back country town . . . Yet I thought nothing of it, so much I delighted in the piety of my father-in-law.*

After one year in Hameln, the young couple moved back to Hamburg and lived with Gluckel's family. There, Hayyim began trading in gold and made a good living. Together, Gluckel and Hayyim had twelve children. Over the course of thirty years, they became one of the most prosperous Jewish families in the city.

Gluckel herself was always active and busy. She worked with Hayyim from their first years. By the time she was twenty-five, the couple had expanded their interests. They began to buy seed pearls. Gluckel maintained this business even after Hayyim died. As she described in her autobiography:

> *. . . I maintained a lively trade in seed pearls. I bought from all the Jews, selected and assorted them, and then resold them in towns where I knew they were in good demand.*

One of the saddest events in Gluckel's long life was the death of her husband, Hayyim. Although she had hardly known him when they married, Gluckel grew to love and respect Hayyim during their thirty years together. Throughout her memoirs, which she began after her husband's death, she referred to him as "my good friend" and "my beloved husband."

As a widow, Guckel faced many problems. She supported her eight unmarried children and had to find suitable mates for them. In addition, one of her sons had fallen into serious debt. She spent a great deal of time and money rescuing him from his creditors and his own foolish mistakes. Gluckel also had to pay her daughters' dowries and often helped her married children financially.

Although she remained prosperous, after more than ten years of widowhood Gluckel began to worry. She had managed to live through wars and expulsions, epidemics and threats to the Jewish community. She had survived the death of a husband and several of her children, but as she grew older she became concerned about how she would maintain herself. As she explained in her memoir:

> *Despite all my pains and traveling about and running from one end of the city to another, I found I could hold out no longer. For though I had a good business and enjoyed large credit . . . I might fall, God forbid, into complete bankruptcy and be compelled to give my creditors all I had, a shame for my children and my pious husband asleep in the earth.*

A drawing of Gluckel of Hameln. The artist and date are unknown.

Gluckel's concerns were realistic. During her lifetime and for many years after, no insurance or government help was available to individuals. Insecurity, worries about money, and loneliness finally helped Gluckel to make a major life decision. On the advice of her son Moses, she married a second time, in 1700. She was fifty-four years old.

Gluckel's new husband was a prosperous banker named Cerf Levy. He had a fine reputation and had been head of the Jewish community of Metz. Gluckel felt she could live out her final years in comfort and security with this man.

Her second marriage started out happily but was not as successful as the first. Cerf was neither as loving nor as honorable as Hayyim had been. Within a few years, he was bankrupt and lost most of Gluckel's money together with his own.

Shortly after this business reversal, Cerf Levy died. Gluckel was alone and penniless. After her husband's debts were paid off, she didn't even have a place to live.

Older and less energetic, Gluckel struggled to remain independent. Determined not to be a burden on her children, she lived in a tiny room in the home of an old friend, Jacob Marburg. Those were the bitterest days of her long life. She wrote:

> *I had neither hearth nor chimney. I had to cook in his kitchen and spend the winter days by his fireside. But when time came to sleep, or for any reason I must go to my room, I had to climb a flight of twenty-two steps. It was so hard for me that usually I abandoned the effort.*

Finally, Gluckel became ill and "could hold out no longer." At the age of seventy, she accepted the invitation of her daughter Esther and her son-in-law Moses. They cared for her lovingly and she spent the last decade of her life happily in their home.

During her final years, Gluckel completed the series of books which she had begun in 1691 when she was forty-five years old. She wrote these books so her children would know about their family. She wanted to be sure that after she died, they would know "from what sort of people" they came.

Gluckel did more than tell her descendants about their roots. After she died in 1724, at the age of seventy-eight, her memoirs were passed around among her children. Written out in seven small notebooks, they were copied several times and were preserved within the family for many generations.

In 1896, Gluckel's book was published in the original Yiddish. Later, it was translated into many languages and read by more people than Gluckel ever dreamed possible. In this first autobiography written by a Jewish woman, we witness Gluckel's unshakable faith in God, and the heroism that enabled her to bounce back from the sorrows of her life.

Rachel Botchan as Hannah Rachel Werbermacher in Miriam Hoffman's play, The Maid of Ludomir, *performed by the Folksbiene Yiddish Theater in New York, 1996.*

Chapter 10

Pious Women: From Rebels to Rebbes

For the Jews of eastern Europe, the seventeenth century was a difficult one. Wars and massacres followed one after the other. Thousands of Jews in Poland, Lithuania, and the Ukraine were murdered.

There were major disappointments within their own communities as well. Shabtai Zvi, a Turkish Jew, promised to usher in a new world of peace and lead the Jewish people back to the land of Israel. Many believed that he was the long-awaited Messiah. They packed their bags and prepared to depart for the "promised land" whenever Shabtai would call. However, threatened with death by the Muslims, Shabtai Zvi converted to Islam in 1666. Thousands of Jews were brokenhearted and disillusioned.

The Jewish communities of eastern Europe needed renewed hope and a fresh outlook on life. Some found it with a different kind of leader: Israel ben Eliezer. Israel was called the *Baal Shem Tov* by his followers, a title that means "Master of a Good Name."

Modern-day Hasidim still follow the old ways. The women always keep their arms and legs covered and wear hats or scarves.

The *Baal Shem Tov*, known as a healer and a holy man, lived from about 1700 to 1760. He founded a new religious movement called Hasidism (pietism). In contrast to the feelings of sadness, despair, and guilt that had infiltrated eastern European Judaism, Hasidism brought joy and optimism back into Jewish life. In addition, the *Baal Shem* taught that God loved the simple, illiterate Jew as much as the talmudic scholar.

This new attitude briefly created a rare opportunity for Jewish women. For centuries, Jewish learning had been stressed as the most holy and honored of all activities. Women, who had not been obliged, and often not even permitted, to study, were therefore excluded from public leadership roles. For a Hasidic leader, though, scholarship was not the most important quality. Hasidic leaders were admired for their magnetic personalities and ability to communicate joy and piety. The new atmosphere gave women a chance to lead, too.

Women greeted these small changes enthusiastically, often with encouragement from men. Although the *Baal Shem Tov* did not believe that women were equal to men, he urged women, along with uneducated men, to participate more fully. After the *Baal Shem's* death, women came to his followers, the local Hasidic *rebbes*. They asked for advice or requested that special prayers be recited for them. They persuaded others to join the movement.

It is difficult to know exactly how many women flocked to Hasidism because of this new philosophy. It is even harder to determine the number of women who actually took leadership roles.

Malkah, the wife of Rabbi Sholom Rokeah, and her daughter Eidele were active in the rabbinic court of Belz. Perele, daughter of Israel of Kozienice, had her own disciples and wore *tzitzit* (ritual fringes), an obligation required only of men. Sarah, the daughter of Joshua Herschel Teumim Frankel, acted as *rebbe* after her husband's death.

Additional reports of those who gained reputations as holy women are scattered throughout Hasidic literature. Legends and stories tell us of a few who accepted the religious duties of men. Other women were well known for their charity and piety.

As the Hasidic movement became more structured, however, renewed stress was placed on study. Gradually, the avenues that had been open to women were once again closed.

Edel and Feige

The first of the great Hasidic women was Edel. Edel was the only daughter of Israel *Baal Shem Tov*. Because of her charm and outgoing personality, she far outshone her brother Zvi-Hirsch, who was withdrawn and sad.

Edel had a special bond with her father, who considered her one of his pupils. Both father and daughter were credited with an ability to cure the sick. It was Edel who accompanied Israel on his travels to other Jewish communities. She was near him in all his prayers and celebrations and cared for him when he was ill.

When Edel grew older, she asked her father whom she would marry. Instead of arranging a traditional marriage for Edel, as was the custom, the *Baal Shem Tov* said: "Your husband is hidden among the scholars who come here. You must wait until a sign points him out to you."

Edel did not have long to wait. The following Simhat Torah she watched while the men danced wildly. This was how they expressed their joy in the holiday and in the holy Torah. Women traditionally did not dance with men, and this had not changed.

As they flew around in a circle, one of the young dancers lost his shoe. He called out: "A maiden will put the shoe on my foot; a mother will rock the babe in her cradle."

Edel and her father both realized that this was the sign they had awaited. The *Baal Shem* signaled to his daughter to replace the young man's shoe. This same man, Yehiel Ashkenazi, became Edel's husband.

Edel and Yehiel had three children. Their two sons, Moses and Baruch, became scholars and writers. However, it was their daughter Feige who inherited her mother's abilities and spirituality. Hasidim admired her as one who "possessed the holy spirit."

Feige married an uneducated man named Simhah and gave birth to a son, Nahman. Nahman ben Simhah, known as Nahman of Bratslav, became a beloved leader of eighteenth century Hasidism. Rabbi Nahman had great respect for his grandmother, Edel. He said: "All the *tzaddikim* (righteous people) believed her to be endowed with divine inspiration, and a woman of great perception." Feige, too, was known for her divine inspiration. She is credited with encouraging her son's Hasidic leanings.

Throughout their lives, Edel and her daughter Feige were dominant figures in the Hasidic movement. Respected for their wisdom and righteousness, they were revered and emulated by succeeding generations of Jewish women.

Hannah Rachel Werbermacher
(The Maid of Ludomir)

Hannah Rachel Werbermacher, born in 1805, was the most famous of all the Hasidic women. Known as the "maid of Ludomir," she was one of the last to emerge from the Hasidic movement before it turned back towards more conservative ways.

Most of the women who became known as Hasidic leaders were from rabbinic families, but

Hannah Rachel Werbermacher was an exception. She was born in Ludomir, Poland and was not a descendent of rabbis or scholars. The only child of a successful businessman, she was given a better than average education in Jewish subjects and was betrothed to a young scholar.

Shortly after her betrothal, Hannah Rachel fell ill. Then her mother died. Hannah Rachel became depressed and spent more and more time alone.

One day, while visiting her mother's grave, Hannah Rachel fainted and remained unconscious for a long time. When she awoke, she told her father that she had been to Heaven. She believed that she was present at a session of the heavenly court and received a new soul. Religious scholars were consulted. They concluded "we do not know whose religious soul is dwelling in this woman."

After her mystical experience, Hannah Rachel emerged with a new religious fervor. She broke her engagement and took on all the religious obligations required of men. She wore *tzitzit* (ritual fringes) under her clothing and put on a *tallit* (prayer shawl) and *tefilin* (phylacteries) to pray.

Hannah Rachel became known as a healer and a miracle worker. People flocked to Ludomir from all over Poland to ask for her advice, listen to her wisdom, and request special blessings. She spent much of her time studying Torah and rabbinic literature.

A small synagogue was built for Hannah Rachel by the Ludomir community with an adjoining apartment. Jews came in large numbers to pray and hear her sermons every Sabbath. Hannah Rachel remained in her apartment and spoke to her followers through an open door so no one would see her. This conformed to the traditional requirement of modesty for women.

When she was forty years old, Hannah Rachel Werbermacher was finally persuaded to marry by Mordecai of Czernobiel, an influential rabbi. He shared the accepted belief that it was unnatural for women to remain unmarried. However, the marriage lasted less than a week before the couple separated.

After this brief marriage, Hannah Rachel's influence waned in Ludomir. She emigrated to Jerusalem where she spent her time studying the Kaballah, a book of Jewish mysticism. She was described by a contemporary as "a short woman, well known by all the citizens of Jerusalem. Each morning she walked to the *Kotel* (the Western Wall of the ancient Temple), carrying her *tallit* and *tefilin*, followed by a throng of elderly individuals who wished to receive her blessing."

During her years in Jerusalem, followers still came to Hannah Rachel to hear her interpret the weekly Torah readings. On Simhat Torah a large crowd gathered outside her home.

Every month, in celebration of Rosh Hodesh (the first day of the month), the "maid of

Ludomir" led a large group of Hasidim to Rachel's tomb for prayers. There, she would collect all the written requests she received from her followers and carefully place them in the cracks of the tomb.

Hannah Rachel enjoyed the respect and love of the many Hasidim who had settled in Jerusalem. She died in 1892, at the age of eighty-seven, admired for her piety and learning.

Hannah Rachel Werbermacher's life spanned almost an entire century. Many changes had occurred during that time. The Jewish ghettos were eliminated and Jews became free to live where they pleased. Secular learning had made many inroads into the Jewish community. Jewish men and women were beginning to study subjects other than Torah and Talmud.

Long before 1892, the year of Hannah Rachel's death, the Hasidim were no longer revolutionary. They emphasized the study of Talmud once more and discouraged the active participation of women in religious ritual. However, the "maid of Ludomir" along with other pious and charismatic women, had helped make Hasidism an important and meaningful religious movement.

A nineteenth century painting of a Polish synagogue, showing a typical woman's gallery (at top).

Chapter 11

A Tradition of Jewish Women Prayer Leaders

In Poland, Lithuania, the Ukraine, and other parts of eastern Europe, Hasidism developed side by side with traditional Jewish learning and observance. As both the Hasidic and the traditional communities expanded, Yiddish — the language that Jews spoke in these lands — became richer and more widespread.

Yiddish did not replace Hebrew, which remained the language of scholarship and prayer, but for those who had no opportunity to learn Hebrew, a whole body of literature and prayers developed in Yiddish. Much of this writing was for women, since they were excluded from studying Hebrew texts.

Often women wrote prayers in their capacity as prayer leaders. These women, referred to in Yiddish as *firzogerins* (foresayers), could be found in almost every congregation in Europe. They were different from the Hasidic women who may have occasionally taken on some of the roles of the *rebbes* and acted as leaders in their small communities. Instead, *firzogerins* led and taught the women in traditional synagogues.

Firzogerins were not new to Jewish life. Dulcie and Urania led the women of the Worms congregation in prayer in the twelfth and thirteenth centuries. In the fifteenth century Devorah Ascarelli did the same in Italy. Rebecca Tiktiner was a *firzogerin* in Prague. They also wrote religious poems and prayers for women.

By the eighteenth century, however, the Yiddish *tehine* had become an accepted literary form. Some *tehines* were simply Hebrew prayers translated into Yiddish or rewritten as Yiddish poetry, but many were completely original. They were written in a very personal and emotional style and dealt with the everyday events and acts of a woman's life. Special prayers were written to recite during the holidays, before candle lighting, and for baking challah. For example, this anonymous prayer asked God:

> *Send an angel to guard the baking so that all will be well baked, will rise nicely, and will not*
>
> *burn, to honor the holy Sabbath . . . over which one recites the holy blessing — as you blessed*
>
> *the dough of Sarah and Rebecca our Mothers.*

There were prayers for times when a family member was sick, or a woman was having a baby. There were prayers for giving to charity. The following prayer was written by an unknown woman:

> *I, your maidservant . . . have taken upon myself, as a vow, to collect funds*
>
> *for charity (tzedakah) and to help the poor and the needy. As God is my*
>
> *witness, I do this with all my heart for the sake of the mitzvah itself and not*
>
> *for honor and recognition . . .*

Unlike the men's prayers, *tehines* were often addressed to the God of our Mothers, Sarah, Rebecca, Rachel, and Leah. These were the biblical heroines with whom women could identify.

Writers of women's prayers such as Leah Horowitz, Sarah bas Tovim, and others who remained anonymous brought spirituality into the lives of Eastern European women. Their prayers were intimate and meaningful. They enabled women to turn their loaves of bread into holy offerings and their kitchens into sanctuaries. Prayers for everyday rituals transformed a woman's daily routines into sacred acts. Today, women scholars are researching and preserving these prayers, recognizing in them a precious legacy.

Sarah bas Tovim

Sarah bas Tovim was the earliest name associated with Yiddish *tehines*. Sarah grew up in the eighteenth century, in the Ukraine, but nothing is known of her roots. Bas Tovim is a pen name that means "daughter of distinguished men," and cannot be traced to any specific family.

Everything we know about Sarah bas Tovim comes from her own writing. Her father, Mordecai, was a scholar and a rabbi. Mordecai's father Isaac was a rabbi as well, and Sarah referred to him as "the great light." His grandfather, also named Mordecai, was head of the rabbinical court of Brisk.

Sarah, too, was well educated. Her writings are filled with biblical and rabbinic quotations, lines from the prayer book, and references to a variety of religious practices. She was born into a prosperous home in the Ukrainian town of Satanov, where she probably served as a prayer leader.

Later in life Sarah was poor and wandered from town to town. This may have been the result of wars and uprisings occurring at that time. Sarah, however, blamed her troubles on her own sins. In one of her prayers, she confessed that while she was young she talked and laughed during prayer services. She also admitted that she came to synagogue wearing fine jewelry in order to show off before the other women. As a result, she was justly punished by homelessness.

"The fact that I am homeless should be a sacrifice for my sins," she wrote. "God Almighty, blessed be He, should forgive me for talking in the Synagogue during services in my youth."

In later years, many prayers and writings were falsely attributed to Sarah bas Tovim. However, two small books were definitely the product of her pen. One is called *Sheker HaHen* (Beauty is Deceptive) and contains prayers for days of fasting. The other, named *Shloyshe Sh'orim* (The Three Gates), became extremely popular during Sarah's lifetime.

Shloyshe Sh'orim is divided into three sections (gates). The first gate includes prayers for the three *mitzvot* women had to perform. These were separating a piece of dough from the challah, lighting the candles, and keeping women's purity (*niddah*). The second gate was a long prayer for Rosh Hodesh (the new month or the new moon), and the third, prayers for the high holidays.

In the prayer for Rosh Hodesh, Sarah bas Tovim describes her idea of Paradise for righteous women. The rewards received by the righteous in Sarah's vision of Paradise reflect the hopes and dreams of the women she knew. In a society where the sexes were separated most of the time, women envisioned Heaven as a place where they would be together with the mothers of Israel and other righteous women.

Sarah describes the six chambers of Heaven reserved for all righteous women. One of these women is Bithiah, daughter of Pharaoh, who pulled Moses from the water. Rejoicing in Moses' accomplishments, she takes pride in the part she played in saving him. Sarah portrays her as saying: "How worthy is my strength and how knowing is my power!"

The poem also recalls other righteous women, including Moses' mother Yocheved, Deborah the prophet, and of course the four mothers of Israel. Sarah writes:

And the chambers of the Mothers cannot be described; no one can come into their chambers.

Now, dear women, when the souls are together in paradise, how much joy there is! Therefore, I pray you to praise God with great devotion, and to say your prayers, that you may be worthy to be there with our Mothers . . .

Sarah bas Tovim died late in the eighteenth century. By the time of her death, she had become a legend in Eastern Europe. She was so well known that long after her death other writers, including men, imitated her style. Sometimes they even signed Sarah's name to their poems. They believed that this would guarantee the acceptance of their *tehines*.

In her writing, Sarah never mentions marriage and does not refer to any children who will carry on her name. However, her work has lived on, long after she herself was forgotten. Sarah bas Tovim's prayers and writings continue to be recited by women in the twentieth century.

Sarah Rebecca Rachel Leah Horowitz

Born at the beginning of the eighteenth century, Sarah Rebecca Rachel Leah Horowitz, usually called Leah, was a contemporary of Sarah bas Tovim. However, it is unlikely that the two ever met. Bas Tovim was from the Ukraine and Horowitz lived in Silesia, a section of Poland.

Horowitz believed that women's prayer had special power to bring the Messiah. She urged women to attend synagogue and to cry. Their tears, she maintained, would help to redeem the Jewish people.

Sarah Rebecca Rachel Leah Horowitz, like so many learned women, was the daughter and the wife of rabbis. In one of her *tehines* she described herself as "daughter of the brilliant and famous rabbi Yokel Segal Horowitz, head of the rabbinical court of Glogau; wife of the brilliant and acute luminary, our teacher Rabbi Shabtai, head of the rabbinical court of Krasny."

One of Leah Horowitz's better-known *tehines* was first published during her lifetime, in the mid-eighteenth century. It was republished in 1796 as part of a pamphlet of Rosh Hodesh prayers. The words of this prayer, called *Tehine of the Mothers*, hint at the difficult times that the Jews of Eastern Europe were experiencing. Leah wrote:

For we have no strength, we can no longer endure the hard, bitter exile, for we are like the feeble lambs.

Several paragraphs further on, she reassured her readers:

We will certainly be called the Daughters of Abraham, the children of Abraham our father, but today we must be in unmerciful hands.

Leah Horowitz was a pious and humble woman. Like Sarah bas Tovim, she also believed that the hard times the Jews were experiencing were a result of their own sins. She prayed to God:

Thoroughly cleanse us of our sins, for we have been thoroughly smitten because of our sins; therefore renew us, and bring us this month to joy . . .

She ended this prayer with a plea, the hope of so many eastern European women in her century:

And we pray You to grant to us . . . worthy, living, and healthy offspring. May they be scholars, and may they serve God with perfect hearts and with love, together with all the pious ones, Amen.

Both Sarah bas Tovim and Leah Horowitz were learned women. Scholars who have analyzed her work, however, believe that Leah Horowitz may have been the most educated of all the women who wrote *tehines*. She was known as a talmudic scholar, a rare accomplishment for Polish Jewish women in the 1700s.

Grace Aguilar

Rachel Luzzatto Morpurgo

Lady Judith Cohen Montefiore

In the nineteenth century these three women tried to balance the new ideas of the Enlightenment with old traditions.

Chapter 12

One Tradition, Many Choices: Enlightened Women of Western Europe

Jewish communities have always adapted to the customs of their host countries. Since the first exile from Judea in 586 B.C.E., Jews have resided in many different lands. In each new place, their life styles and religious practices changed a little. The languages they spoke, the clothes they wore, the work they did, all reflected the cultures in which they lived. However, there was always a core of common rituals and holiday observances, and a shared language of prayer. Most Jews valued education in Torah and maintained a strong social separation from non-Jews.

Beginning in the eighteenth century, that common core of beliefs altered. This was because of a new movement that spread across all of Europe called *The Enlightenment*.

As a result of the new ideas of enlightened philosophers, Jews were allowed to return to many of the lands that had expelled them centuries earlier. Together with Christians in these countries, Jews were being emancipated.

Emancipation began in England in the late seventeenth century and slowly moved eastward. France gave its Jews full civil rights after the French Revolution of 1791. The Austro-Hungarian Empire followed. In 1812, the Edict of Emancipation gave new rights to many of Germany's Jews.

This meant that the Jews were liberated by law from political and religious restrictions. They could act in society with the same rights and duties as other people. Jews were now citizens and were allowed to send their children to public schools. They could apply for government jobs and engage in occupations that were once forbidden to them. For the first time since the era of the Roman Empire, Jews had to act as individuals, because secular governments no longer granted official recognition to their communities.

At first, this seemed to be an advantage for Jews. They could decide for themselves whether they wanted to practice Judaism and how they would educate their children. In the spirit of individual freedom, many Jews embraced non-religious education. This new movement toward modern, scientific schooling led some Jews to question and reject the old ways of their parents.

Others, like Judith Montefiore, saw the dangers of Enlightenment and tried to balance new ideas with old traditions.

Lady Judith Cohen Montefiore

Judith Cohen was born in London, England, late in the 1700s. The Cohens were wealthy merchants, originally from Holland, and they educated their daughter in both Jewish and secular subjects. Judith studied languages, music, singing, drawing, and English literature, as well as the Hebrew Bible and the prayer book.

On June 10, 1812, Judith Cohen, of Ashkenazi descent, married Moses Montefiore, a Sephardic Jew and a successful businessman. Although the bride and groom came from different cultural backgrounds, it was considered an excellent match. Judith confided to her diary:

I was this day united in the holy bonds of matrimony to Moses Montefiore, whose fraternal and filial affection . . . which, joined to many other good qualities and attention toward me, ripened into a more ardent sentiment.

Lady Judith Cohen Montefiore was a philanthropist and a world traveler.

Although she was careful to use the most proper language, Judith was in love. She affectionately called her new husband "Monte" and was devoted and loyal to him until her death.

Living in a more tolerant world than most other Jews outside of England, Judith and Moses were not strictly observant. Many of their activities would have been frowned on by the more traditional Jews of eastern Europe. Judith enjoyed games of whist, appeared at charity and state balls, and attended the opera.

However, the couple remained firmly attached to their faith. Moses was knighted by Queen Victoria in recognition of his service to the Jewish community. From then on, Judith was referred to by the title "Lady." Because of her many fine qualities, she became one of the most loved and admired women among England's Jews.

At a time when Jews were drifting away from the synagogue, and few women attended services, Judith went regularly. She influenced her husband to do the same. Three days after her wedding she wrote in her diary:

> *I do not know any circumstance more pleasing to me than to perceive that my dear Monte is religiously inclined.*

Lady Montefiore attended the synagogue throughout her lifetime. In her frequent travels to other countries, she often expressed regret at the small number of women who came to pray.

Judith demonstrated her religious commitment with charitable work as well as prayer. She had no children of her own, but focused on the care of orphans and the education of girls. Together, the Montefiores were involved in raising money for Jewish causes, both in England and the Holy Land (Palestine).

Because travel in the nineteenth century was difficult and dangerous, almost no women went on long journeys. In spite of this, Lady Montefiore fulfilled a lifelong dream and accompanied her husband to Palestine in 1827. At that time she noted in her diary that "only six European females are said to have visited Palestine in the course of the century."

On their trips to the Holy Land the Montefiores had to travel much of the way by coach and horses. They crossed mountains and deserts where no roads had yet been built. Because of the war between Greece and Turkey, sailing the Mediterranean was often perilous. Once on land, there were highwaymen who preyed on travelers. Poor lodgings were rat-infested, and there was the ever-present danger of plague in the Middle East. Judith was always thankful when they reached Palestine safely.

During their first trip, Judith and Moses Montefiore realized how poor the small settlements of Jews were. Many of the men were religious and spent their days in study. They depended on the charity of rich European Jews to survive, plus the little their wives might earn by sewing, laundering, or other services. For those who were ready to work, there were almost no jobs. After centuries of exile, Jews knew nothing of farming.

Moses Montefiore conceived an exciting plan. He and Judith would help to develop agriculture in the Jewish settlements of Palestine. In this way, they believed, poor Jews would be able to become self-sufficient and not depend on charity.

By their second trip, undertaken in 1838, Judith was already well known and admired among

Palestine's Jews. When they went to synagogue in Jerusalem, she was granted "the singular honor of lighting four lamps in front of the altar and putting the bells on the *Sefer.*" In this traditional synagogue, where men and women were separated, and women were not permitted to touch the Torah, this was indeed an extraordinary event.

Judith and Moses visited the Holy Land again in 1855. They gave a great deal of money to help build the first agricultural settlement outside the walls of Jerusalem. It was called *Yemin Moshe*, after Moses (*Moshe* in Hebrew) Montefiore.

Between their journeys, Moses and Judith lived in Ramsgate, England, where Judith died in 1862. As a memorial, her beloved husband founded a college in Judith's name, devoted to the pursuit of Jewish studies. This seems a fitting memorial for Lady Judith Cohen Montefiore. She used her time, her position, and her wealth to further the cause of the Jewish people in England and in Palestine.

Rachel Luzzatto Morpurgo

Rachel Luzzatto Morpurgo was the first woman to write modern Hebrew poetry. Her work reflects both traditional Jewish life and the enlightened ideas of the emancipation. Although she emphasized Jewish values, Rachel's poems expressed her own experiences and emotions. They were not written in the form of prayers, nor were they meant to be recited in the synagogue.

Rachel was born in Trieste on April 8, 1790. Her parents were prosperous and respected in the community. One branch of an important and scholarly family of Italian Jews, the Luzzattos had settled in Trieste while it was still part of Italy. By the time of Rachel's birth, Trieste had been added to the Austro-Hungarian Empire.

The family gave Rachel the same excellent education that her brother and her male cousins received. The Luzzatto children never went to a formal school, but studied at home with their learned uncles.

Rachel was first taught to read the Bible and commentaries in the original Hebrew. By the age of twelve, she was able to understand many popular Hebrew works. At fourteen she began the study of Talmud and Rashi's commentaries. She also learned lithography and dressmaking from family members. However, poetry was what she loved best. She began writing at the age of eighteen and did not stop until her death at eighty-one.

As a young woman, Rachel refused all of the suitors approved by her family. Instead, she insisted on a man of her own choosing: Jacob Morpurgo. Jacob was an Austrian Jew who made a modest living as a merchant.

It was very uncommon for young Jewish women to choose their own husbands in the early years of the nineteenth century. Rachel's parents opposed the match for many years. They preferred a scholarly and wealthy husband for their daughter, but Rachel lived at the beginning of a new era and refused to marry a man just because her parents had chosen him. When she was twenty-nine years old, Rachel's parents finally consented and her marriage to Jacob was celebrated.

Rachel and Jacob Morpurgo had three sons and one daughter. Her family life kept her busy, but she always managed to find time for poetry. Many of her poems were published in a Hebrew journal called *Stars of Isaac*. Her work was admired by Jews who understood Hebrew, and she had a small but devoted following.

As she grew older, Rachel began to believe in mysticism, the idea of the union of the soul with God through contemplation and love. Her poems are filled with images of souls reaching up to heaven, and hopes for the coming of the Messiah. The language is lyrical and spiritual. In one of her later works she wrote:

Rachel Luzzatto Morpurgo of Trieste composed poetry in Hebrew.

> I watch the eternal hills, the far, far lying,
>
> With glorious flowers ever over-run;
>
> I take me eagles' wings, with vision flying
>
> And brow upraised to look upon the sun.

Rachel Luzzatto Morpurgo died in 1871, loved and respected as a modern Hebrew poet. To honor her after her death, her poems were collected and published in 1890. In 1923, they were translated by Nina Davis

Salaman, an English Jewish scholar and poet. With this publication Rachel Morpurgo was brought to life for a new generation of Jews.

The Berlin Salon Women

The Jews of Germany were not fully emancipated until the nineteenth century. Yet long before emancipation, a large number of Jews were strongly influenced by the ideas of the Enlightenment, sometimes called the Age of Reason. Most of them were wealthy and lived in Berlin, the cultural center of Germany. Some converted and intermarried. This was encouraged by the Christian community and was a path into the new and exciting society from which German Jews were still excluded.

In the mid-1700s, a leading German Jew, Moses Mendelssohn, tried to change this trend. He was convinced that Jews could be accepted in German society and still maintain Jewish life.

Moses Mendelssohn himself succeeded in this. He was considered an example of the new Jew: religiously observant, and also well educated and ruled by Reason. However, he failed to stop the movement towards conversion and assimilation. After his death in 1786, Mendelssohn's own son Abraham had his children baptized and raised as Christians. Moses' daughters, Henrietta and Dorothea, converted to Catholicism.

Henrietta and Dorothea Mendelssohn presided over active salons. In their own living rooms (salons) they gathered artists, poets, and educated members of the German nobility. These men were eager to exchange ideas and share progressive opinions.

Dorothea Mendelssohn was one of the more famous of the salon women. Others included Henrietta De Lemos Herz and Rahel Levin Varnhagen. They came from rich families and were given fine secular educations. Sometimes, their Jewish educations were neglected. Surrounded by anti-Jewish attitudes, they felt increasingly negative about Judaism.

Salon women like Dorothea, Henrietta, and Rahel were charming, intelligent, and socially skilled. With their guests they found an outlet for their creativity. The informal salon gatherings also offered a way of meeting the best of Berlin's high society. Some of Germany's greatest philosophers and thinkers were recognized and encouraged by the Berlin salon women.

Most of the Jewish salon women had been married to Jewish men when still very young. Following the old custom, these marriages were arranged by their parents. Sometimes their husbands were much older and had little in common with their talented and lively wives.

By contrast, the salons were frequented by younger, more modern Christian men who offered admiration and friendship. Sometimes, a specific friendship grew into love. A few

Jewish women may also have seen marriage to such men as a chance to be accepted into upper class German society.

Dorothea Mendelssohn left her Jewish husband and ran off to France with Frederick von Schlegel, a gentile philosopher and writer. In Paris, Dorothea converted to marry Frederick legally. She died as a Catholic in 1839.

Rahel Levin was engaged twice to Christian men, but both times the engagement was broken. Finally, at the age of forty-one, she converted in order to marry Karl August Varnhagen.

A Christian nobleman, Varnhagen was fourteen years younger than Rahel. He had little money and became a minor government official. The greatest German intellectuals and writers of the time, such as Goethe, Heine, and Schleiermacher continued to gather in Rahel's Berlin salon.

Rahel Levin Varnhagen struggled with her feelings toward Judaism all her life. She was not religious and never observed Jewish rituals. Still, she confessed in her memoirs, it was very difficult for her to convert.

Rahel may have regretted her decision, at least in her later years. As she lay dying, in 1833, she said to her husband: "What for such a long period of my life was my greatest shame, my bitterest suffering and misfortune — to have been born a Jewess — I would not now have missed at any price."

Henrietta Mendelssohn, Dorothea's sister, remained single all her life. She moved from Berlin to Vienna, where she became a governess. Later she headed a boarding school in Paris. She converted to Catholicism after the death of her parents.

Henrietta De Lemos Herz was married at the age of fifteen to a Jewish doctor seventeen years older than herself. Although the couple stayed together, they had little in common. Henrietta did not convert, but became estranged from Judaism. She tried to explain the reason for this in one passage of her diary:

> The children, particularly the girls, were not at all really instructed in the faith of their parents . . . Their parents didn't want to teach them what they, themselves, did not believe and so they were (and are) raised with no faith . . . Reason, which the culture takes as their help and support, does not suffice them in severe suffering.

The Berlin salons lasted only a brief time. They were at their height in the last few decades of the 1700s. By 1806, when France invaded and occupied Berlin, they all but disappeared. However, in this short period of time, a handful of Jewish women influenced their world and shaped the ideas of a changing society.

By the nineteenth century new forms of Judaism were developing in Germany to combat the trend toward conversion. The Reform Movement was organized to help German Jews maintain some Jewish tradition as they moved into the modern world. Conservative Judaism developed shortly afterwards, offering still another choice to Jews. Jews who conformed to traditional practices called themselves Orthodox but tried to infuse the old ways with new meanings.

Such options gave Jewish women a broader choice than the salon women ever had. Although a few women continued to see no future for themselves within the Jewish community, most remained devoted to Judaism. Many educated Jewish women used their knowledge to bring Jewish history and Jewish moral lessons into the lives of others.

Grace Aguilar

Grace Aguilar was an English Jew of Sephardic origin who wanted Jewish women to take pride in their faith. She believed that women should enjoy social as well as spiritual equality. The many books she wrote were directed toward Jewish women. She urged them to embrace what she considered the true meaning of Judaism.

Grace, a descendent of *Marranos*, was born in London in 1816. She was well educated in Judaism and was taught Hebrew. While still young, she helped her mother run a school to support the family.

Through contact with young people, Grace became aware of the turmoil among Jewish youth, particularly girls. She understood how modern thinking undermined traditional Jewish life. In her book *The Jewish Faith* she tried to offer "the spiritual consolation, moral guidance, and immortal hope of Judaism." Personal prayer, she explained, was "the language of the heart" and "the hour of communion between the individual and God." Judaism was a "living faith," Grace insisted, and the Jewish God was a "God of love, justice and mercy." The book was written in the form of letters to a young girl who had little Jewish education.

Aguilar felt that Jewish women needed to understand the Hebrew Bible and know the great women in the biblical stories. To meet that need, she wrote a two-volume work entitled *Women of Israel: Characters and Sketches from the Holy Scriptures and Jewish History*.

Grace particularly encouraged mothers to teach their children "the religion of the heart." She felt that women, even more than men, needed a feeling of closeness to God. This religious feeling would help them through the many trials they faced in life.

Despite poor health, Grace wrote and studied throughout her brief life. She penned every word of her lengthy books by hand. Most of them were written in a short span of seven years, from 1840 until her death.

Grace Aguilar, an English author, wrote many books for Jewish women.

Aguilar died in 1847, at the age of 31. She produced at least eight books as well as articles and poetry. She also translated the works of others from Hebrew into English.

Grace Aguilar had a loyal following in England and also in America. She corresponded with Rabbi Isaac Leeser, leader of the Jews of Philadelphia. Leeser was the founder of the Jewish Publication Society, and he arranged to have her works published in the United States.

The following excerpt from a letter written to Grace Aguilar shows the grateful reactions of the women who read her books.

> *You, dearest Sister . . . have taught us to know and appreciate our dignity . . . You have vindicated our social and spiritual equality with our brethren in the faith . . . Your writings place within our reach those higher motives . . . which flow from the spirituality of our religion.*

During her life and after her death, Grace Aguilar was one of the most famous Jewish cultural figures of the early nineteenth century. Her books were widely read and she was admired by Jews and Christians throughout the world.

Pauline Wengeroff

Other Jewish women also attempted to hold back the tide of assimilation that was sweeping over the Jews of Europe. From England all across the continent to Russia, Jewish women were facing similar problems and struggling to find solutions. One such woman was Pauline Wengeroff.

Born in Bobruisk, Belorussia in 1833, Pauline witnessed the loss of religious commitment among much of Russia's middle class Jewry. Her father, Judah Epstein, was a wealthy merchant and scholar. Her husband, Hanan Wengeroff, was a banker from Minsk. The couple had two sons and three daughters.

After Pauline's marriage, she kept a diary, a common pastime for women of that period. In it, she recorded personal details as well as political events. She described how Jewish attitudes changed after the Enlightenment spread to Russia. The tolerant rulings of Tzar Alexander II offered new opportunities to Jews and gave rise to new problems.

"After the Polish uprising of 1863," Pauline wrote, "Jewish studies (in Jewish schools) were shortened to make more time for the general curriculum." In those years, there was conflict and bitterness between parents and children; between those who followed the older traditions and those, like Pauline's husband, who preferred modern ways.

Pauline Wengeroff was heartbroken by this transformation of Jewish life. However, she was powerless to alter her husband's decisions. Regretfully, she followed him into the modern world. At his insistence, she gradually left behind many of the Jewish traditions that she loved. She no longer wore the wig which was the mark of pious women. She stopped keeping a kosher kitchen. In trying to preserve the cherished traditions for herself and her children she "fought a battle of life and death."

Then in March 1881, Tzar Alexander II was assassinated. This caused a powerful reaction against all his policies. Tzar Alexander's son and successor, Alexander III, was convinced that the rebellion was the result of his father's enlightened ideas. He withdrew all recently acquired Jewish rights to education and denied Jews the opportunity to live in the larger cities. Gangs of gentiles prowled the streets, assaulting Jews, and anti-Semitism reached a new high. Many Jews emigrated. Others converted.

Wengeroff recalled her mother's words: "Two things I know for certain. I and my generation will surely live and die as Jews. Our grandchildren will surely live and die not as Jews."

This prediction was at least partially fulfilled. Pauline's two sons both converted. She records that this event was "the hardest blow of my life." She mourned it not only as a mother but as "a Jewess mourning for the Jewish people that has lost so many of its noblest sons."

Wengeroff's diary, *Memoirs of a Grandmother*, was written in German, the language of the Enlightenment. It was published between 1908 and 1910. Following in her footsteps, her children were all involved in the world of books and literature.

Pauline Wengeroff died in 1916, just one year before the Communist Revolution ended tzarist rule. At that time large numbers of Jewish youth embraced the non-religious culture of the new Soviet Union. They turned their backs on Judaism and forgot the struggles of the past. Wengeroff's *Memoirs of a Grandmother* remains the only Russian Jewish work of this period written by a woman that recalls these struggles. It is a moving account of the experiences of her generation.

Annie Nathan Meyer, founder of Barnard College, was a rebel all her life.

Chapter 13

Women of the New World

In the same year that Jews were expelled from Spain (1492), Christopher Columbus set out on his voyage of discovery. The new continent he found eventually became a haven for many different people, including Jews.

The first Jews to arrive in the Western Hemisphere were *Sephardim*. They fled Portugal and its Inquisition for the safety of the Dutch settlement in Recife, Brazil. When Portugal took control of Recife, however, and the Inquisition spread from Spain and Portugal to their colonies, a handful of Jews escaped once more.

Sailing north in a small boat, twenty-three refugees arrived in the port of New Amsterdam in 1654. They were the first group of Jews to settle in North America.

From such beginnings, a Jewish community was built. By 1729 New Amsterdam had become New York City, in the English colony of New York, and the first synagogue building was erected. This synagogue was followed by others in cities such as Newport, Rhode Island; Philadelphia, Pennsylvania; and Charleston, South Carolina. In 1776, when the American Revolution broke out, 2,500 Jews were living in the thirteen colonies.

Most Jews sided with the colonists against England. Not surprisingly, the names we hear most often are those of men. Hayyim Solomon is considered a great revolutionary hero, as are Isaac Franks and Philip Minis.

These were not the only Jewish heroes of the Revolution, though. Another was Esther Etting Hayes, of Westchester, New York. Her husband and son were fighting in the colonial army and she, too, wanted to do her part. She managed to cross enemy lines with much-needed salt and supplies hidden beneath her petticoats. Even after her house was burned by the British, she continued smuggling. She repeatedly risked imprisonment, even death, but she was never caught.

Abigail Minis was known as the mother of the Jewish community of Savannah, Georgia. After her husband, Abraham, died in 1757, she managed his extensive business and raised her eight children alone.

When the Revolutionary War broke out, Abigail was already in her eighties. However, she actively supplied the revolutionary army with much-needed goods. Known as a committed supporter of the Revolution, she was forced to flee when Savannah was captured by the British.

Abigail's son Philip helped the Americans recapture the city by furnishing information to the commanding officers. After the war, Abigail Minis returned to Georgia with her five unmarried daughters and lived out the remainder of her life in Savannah. She died there at the age of ninety-six.

When the Revolution was over, President George Washington officially welcomed Jewish citizens into the United States of America. Jews settled down and began building in their new land.

Many women lived lives of quiet heroism during those early years. They struggled to raise Jewish children in areas without synagogues and, sometimes, with no other Jews. A few women recognized the needs of these Jewish families. They worked to create institutions and strengthen Jewish communities.

A painting of

Rebecca Gratz by an

American artist.

Rebecca Gratz

Rebecca Gratz was the sixth of ten children. Her father's family had originated in Poland, but immigrated to America from England in the 1750s. Rebecca was born in Philadelphia in 1781, just after the Revolutionary War.

Michael Gratz, Rebecca's father, was a successful merchant. He ran a shipping business and also traded with the Native Americans in western Pennsylvania and Kentucky. Gratz was one of the founders of Mikveh Israel, the first synagogue established in Pennsylvania.

With her sisters and brothers, Rebecca grew up in the refined society of upper class Philadelphia. She was well educated in secular as well as Jewish subjects, but her commitment to Judaism never wavered. Rumors that she loved a Christian man, Samuel Ewing, were never confirmed. No one knows whether her refusal to marry was due solely to her attachment to Judaism or was the result of her desire to remain independent.

Rebecca directed her time and money toward organizing the first women's charities in Philadelphia. Most of these societies were devoted to helping poor women and orphaned children. Rebecca moved in Christian as well as Jewish circles. We know about her life through the letters she wrote to relatives and friends.

Many people believed that she was the model for the Jewish character, Rebecca, in Sir Walter Scott's popular novel *Ivanhoe*. Gratz had read the book and mentioned in a letter to her sister-in-law: "I am glad you admire Rebecca, for she is just such a representation of a good girl as I think human nature can reach."

Influenced partly by the writings of Grace Aguilar and Penina Moise (see below), Rebecca was determined to pass on her Jewish heritage. In 1838, with the encouragement of Isaac Leeser, rabbi of Mikveh Israel, she founded The Hebrew Sunday School Society. Most of the students were children from the Jewish working class who attended public schools.

For the first time, girls and boys studied religion together in these Sunday School classes. Gratz even hired women as teachers, a radical change from traditional Jewish education. Rebecca headed the Sunday School for more than twenty-five years. It became a model for other schools throughout the country.

Gratz's activities took her out of the confines of her own home and family into a broader world. She lived a public life, deeply committed to the Jewish community. At the time of her death in 1869, Rebecca Gratz was revered as one of the foremost Jewish women in America.

Penina Moise

Charleston, South Carolina was home to another growing and active Jewish community. It was to this safe haven that the Moise family escaped after a slave uprising in the West Indies in 1791. Penina Moise was born in Charleston on April 23, 1797.

Penina was only twelve years old when her father died. Although not the oldest, she assumed the task of caring for her sick mother and younger siblings. Penina was forced to leave school and help support her family by doing needlework. Nevertheless, she always made time to study and write. When she was older, she ran a girls' school together with her sister and her niece. Like many other notable women of this century, Penina Moise did not marry.

Penina's first poems were published while she was still very young. In fact, she was the first Jew to publish lyric poetry in the United States. By the time she was thirty, Moise was a well-known and respected poet. In 1835 a collection of her poems was published under the title *Fancy's Sketch Book*.

Penina was a member of Charleston's literary circle and one of its cultural leaders. She hosted a literary salon in her home where writers met regularly.

Moise also inspired others by her devotion to Judaism. When she became superintendent of Temple Beth Elohim's Sunday School, Penina was one of the first women in America to hold such an important post.

In her later years, Penina wrote many hymns for the congregation to sing. Some are still included in the Reform prayer book. Eventually, Temple Beth Elohim compiled Moise's hymns and published the entire collection.

Penina never retreated from any job that had to be done. During a yellow fever epidemic in 1854, she volunteered in the hospitals. At great risk to her own health, she nursed the sick and dying. Penina records this experience in one of her poems. Her writing also reflects the broader issues of her day: freedom, immigration, and the status of women.

Penina Moise,

the first American

Jewish poet,

also wrote hymns

for her congregation.

Shortly after the Civil War ended, Penina Moise began to lose her eyesight. Nevertheless, she continued to write poetry. Some of her most beautiful and moving hymns were written during this period. In one prayer, which she called "Aspiration," she wrote:

> *Let wisdom of the heart, O Lord!*
> *Be now and ever mine;*
> *Naught else is life's sublime reward,*
> *We love Thy law divine.*

When she died in 1880, at the age of eighty-three, Penina Moise was totally blind. The epitaph on her tombstone reads:

> *Lay no flowers on my grave.*
> *They are for those who live in the sun,*
> *And I have always lived in the shadow.*

Many Jews still sing her hymns today. Through her poetry Penina Moise continues to inspire new generations of Jews.

Ernestine Potowski Rose

Ernestine Potowski was born in Piotrkow, an obscure little town in Poland, on January 13, 1810. She became a famous speaker and an advocate for women's rights in America — the first Jew to actively embrace the cause of women's suffrage (right to vote) in this country.

Ernestine, a rabbi's daughter, was a rebel from her earliest years. She constantly challenged the rules and demands of her small Jewish community.

After her mother's death, her father, without consulting her, arranged for Ernestine to marry a much older man. Only sixteen years old, Ernestine was horrified, but she had nowhere to turn to appeal her father's decision. In her town of Piotrkow, the Jews still depended on their rabbi when they needed advice. That rabbi was her father!

Desperate, Ernestine made the long journey to the nearest city and took her case to the Polish courts. The judge ruled that the contract her father had made was not binding. Ernestine Potowski need not marry. Furthermore, she, and not her intended husband, had the right to her mother's inheritance.

With this legal assurance, Ernestine returned home but did not stay long. Taking only a small part of the money that was rightfully hers, she left Poland and her father forever.

During her short stays in Germany and France, Ernestine Potowski managed to support herself, partly by tutoring in German and Hebrew. She continued on to England, searching for a country with more freedom and individual rights.

In England, Ernestine joined a group headed by Robert Owen. Owen believed that ordinary people, working together, could create a perfect society (utopia). No one would be very rich, but poverty would be eliminated.

It was in England that Ernestine met her husband, William Rose, a silversmith and a committed Owenite. Soon after their marriage, Ernestine and William left for the United States.

In 1836, when the Roses first arrived in New York City, many reform groups were organizing, in an effort to improve society. Ernestine joined the Abolitionists, a group that worked to abolish slavery. She was the only Jewish woman who became well known as a speaker against slavery during that time. She also became part of the small group of women and men who were struggling to pass the Married Women's Property Act.

The law in the United States at that time stated that once a woman married, everything she owned became the property of her husband. This led to many abuses and problems. Supporters of the Married Women's Property Act said that women should have the right to own property in their own names even after they were married.

In the early part of the nineteenth century, most people were against the Married Women's Property Act. They felt it would contribute to the breakup of families. Because of her early experiences in Poland, Ernestine knew how important it was for women to control their own lives. She immediately became involved in working to pass the bill.

Slowly, her causes gained support. In 1848, the Married Women's Property Act was passed in New York State. Partly through the efforts of Ernestine and other women, the Abolitionist Movement had also grown considerably in the North. The national government was feeling increasing pressure to put an end to slavery.

The year 1848 saw another important event as well. The first Women's Rights Convention was held that year in Seneca Falls, a small town in upstate New York. Ernestine Rose joined this group of committed women. She soon became friends with the founders, Elizabeth Cady Stanton, Lucretia Mott, and later, Susan B. Anthony.

Ernestine Rose was one of the principal speakers for the Women's Movement from 1848 until she returned to England in 1869. Known as "the queen of the lecture platform," she spoke at every major conference on women's rights and the abolition of slavery. Everywhere she went, Ernestine met with controversy and opposition. But when she finished speaking, audiences usually gave her a standing ovation.

Ernestine Potowski Rose gave up practicing Judaism when she left her father's home. She married a non-Jew. She never denied that she was Jewish, though. When the editor of an important newspaper in Boston wrote an editorial condemning Jews as "the worst people of whom we have any account," Ernestine was quick to respond. Jews are well settled in major cities, she wrote and "no calamity has yet befallen any place in consequence of that fact." She insisted: "wherever they are they act just about the same as other people."

During the thirty-three years that Ernestine and William lived in the United States, they saw many changes. In 1860 the Emancipation Proclamation ended slavery. Shortly after the Civil War, Congress amended the Constitution to give all African-American men the right to vote.

After the Married Women's Property Act was passed, many other new laws helped women towards equality. Women who worked were given the right to keep their own salaries. They were granted the right to sue in court — even to sue their husbands. New laws gave women joint guardianship over their children. Until then, this right had belonged only to fathers.

Ernestine rejoiced over the progress that had been made, but she never stopped working for the ultimate goal: true equality for all women and the right to vote. She traveled tirelessly throughout the country, lecturing at meetings and conferences.

Finally, broken in health and exhausted, Ernestine, with her husband William Rose, returned

to England in 1869. There, she lived out the remainder of her life.

Among those who paid written tribute to Ernestine Rose before she left the United States was Jonas Bondi. Bondi was editor of the Jewish newspaper *The Hebrew Leader*. He referred to Mrs. Rose as "the earliest and noblest among the workers in the cause of human enfranchisement." Of all those who had fought for human freedom and social progress, he said, none had exhibited more "constancy, devotion, sacrifice, earnestness and ability than Ernestine L. Rose."

Ernestine Rose was known in America as the "Queen of the Lecture Platform."

Ernestine's rheumatic illness became progressively worse in England. When Susan B. Anthony requested that she record something about her life for a history of the Women's Movement, she could only offer a brief reply:

All I can tell you is, that I used my humble powers to the uttermost, and raised my voice in behalf

of human rights in general, and the elevation of women in particular, nearly all my life.

At the age of eighty-two, Ernestine Rose died peacefully and was buried next to her husband. At the grave, a friend said of her: "In her youth, her dark hair and gleaming eyes showed she had the fire of Judith in her." He continued: "The slaves she helped to free from the bondage of ownership, and the minds she had set free from the bondage of authority, were the glad and proud remembrance of her last days."

Emma Lazarus

When Emma Lazarus was born, on July 22, 1849, Ernestine Rose had been on the lecture circuit for more than ten years. The Women's Rights Movement was just beginning, and the Civil War would soon threaten America's very existence — but Emma Lazarus lived a sheltered life, far from the politics raging all around her.

Emma was the fifth child of Moses and Esther Nathan Lazarus, prosperous Sephardic Jews. Her mother was of English descent, but her father, Moses, could trace his ancestry back to the first twenty-three Jews who settled in New York in 1654. Raised in the rich society of uptown Manhattan, Emma was part of an elite world of private education, elegant homes, and literary salons.

Always fragile and sickly, Emma Lazarus studied at home. She was educated in languages and the classics and loved books. Emma began writing poetry as a child, and when she was seventeen years old, her work was published by her admiring father. Although intended to be read only by the family, Emma's poems caught the attention of others and were soon republished. Her early success encouraged her to write more poetry and then a novel.

Emma never married and did not need to work to support herself. Instead, she devoted her life to literature. Ralph Waldo Emerson, the great American essayist and philosopher, was one of Emma's mentors. He read her works, made suggestions, and praised her successes.

As a young girl, Emma was extremely shy and had few friends her own age. Rumors that she loved her handsome and wild cousin, Washington Nathan, were never confirmed. Although the rumors persist to this day, none of her writings suggest there is any truth to these reports.

Some of her early work did touch on Jewish themes, but Lazarus' serious commitment to her people came later. Emma was thirty-two years old when she first saw the Russian Jewish refugees who had escaped the pogroms in Eastern Europe. At first, she could hardly believe that they were Jews. Poor, sick, dirty, and uneducated, they were very different from the Jews that she knew.

Overcoming her shyness, Emma visited the immigrants often. She went to Castle Garden, where the new arrivals were screened, and visited them in

Emma Lazarus, an American poet, became an activist for needy Jewish immigrants.

their homes. She brought money, food, and clothing for the destitute refugees and soon organized groups to train Jews in industrial trades. This project grew into the Hebrew Technical Institute.

Emma attended rallies to raise money for Russian Jews and wrote about them in poems and essays. As she eloquently pointed out: "Until we are all free, we are none of us free."

Hers was a courageous stand in 1881. At that time, many American Jews were afraid to associate with these poor immigrants. They feared the newcomers would reflect badly on their own community, which had so recently struggled for equality and respect in the United States. Some even suggested that America should not accept these "different" Jews.

Rejecting this view, Emma championed Jewish unity and began to feel a growing commitment to the Jewish people. In order to learn more about her culture, she decided to study Hebrew. By her own initiative Emma became one of the more learned Jewish scholars of her time. She was the foremost translator of the poems of Judah HaLevi and Solomon ibn Gabirol, two great Spanish Hebrew poets of the Middle Ages.

Perhaps influenced by these Jewish poets, Emma became sympathetic to Zionism. This cause was not at all popular in the American Jewish community of the nineteenth century. In a poem designed to alert her people to the cause of Zionism and urge them to work for a return to the Jewish homeland in Palestine, she wrote:

> *Wake, Israel, wake! Recall today*
>
> *The glorious Maccabean rage.*
>
> *. . . Oh, for Jerusalem's trumpets now*
>
> *To blow a blast of shattering power,*
>
> *To wake the sleepers high and low,*
>
> *And rouse them to the urgent hour!*

One of Lazarus' most familiar poems is also one of her last. Written shortly before her premature death, it was donated to an auction held to raise funds for the Statue of Liberty.

The statue, a gift from France, was being delivered to the United States. America needed a pedestal on which to place it. One means of raising funds for that pedestal was a public auction of the works of American poets and artists.

Emma wrote and contributed "The New Colossus." It ended with the stirring lines:

. . . Give me your tired, your poor,

Your huddled masses yearning to breathe free,

The wretched refuse of your teeming shore.

Send these, the homeless, tempest-tossed to me.

I lift my lamp beside the golden door.

Emma Lazarus was not present when her work, along with that of other American poets, was auctioned off. She died in 1887, a victim of cancer at the age of 38. Not until 1903 was her poem engraved on a metal plaque and attached to the pedestal of the Statue of Liberty. Since then, it has been memorized by countless school children, translated into many languages, put to music, and recited everywhere.

Through the power of her words, Emma Lazarus helped create the image of America as a haven for the oppressed.

Annie Nathan Meyer

Annie Nathan was Emma Lazarus' first cousin. Her father, Robert Weeks Nathan, was a younger brother of Emma Lazarus' mother. Although both Annie and Emma were of Sephardic descent, and considered wealthy, their lives were very different. Annie was born in 1867, almost twenty years after her cousin. And unlike the Lazarus family, who lived quiet and secluded lives, scandal followed Annie Nathan's family wherever they went.

Annie's mother, Annie Florance, came from another distinguished Sephardic family that "had a drinking problem." Both her parents had love affairs with other people — behavior considered shocking by the Victorian society of upper class New York City. Robert Nathan was also plagued with financial difficulties.

Annie was eleven years old when her mother died. Her sister Maud was only sixteen. However, the girls still had their father, and were surrounded by grandparents, uncles, aunts, and cousins. They received the same kind of education as other Nathan children and lived an upper class society life, with governesses and servants.

In her autobiography, Annie wrote that from the time she was a little girl, she had always wanted to go to college. Her father explained to her that men hated intelligent women, and if she went to college she would never marry.

Although it echoed a common belief of the time, this dire warning did not stop Annie. Many of the young men she knew were attending Columbia University, a school for men only. There was a special "Collegiate Course" at Columbia, designed for women, and Annie enrolled. However, as one writer reported, "it was devoted . . . to teaching women to roll hems and balance teacups."

Disappointed, Annie dropped out of Columbia's Collegiate Course at the age of twenty and looked for another school. There were no institutions in the entire city of New York, or even in nearby areas, that offered a college education for women. The following year Annie Nathan married Alfred Meyer, a successful New York doctor. However, she did not forget about her early dreams of education.

Shortly after her marriage, Annie decided to start a women's college in New York City. She began to raise money among her many relatives and acquaintances. Every day, Annie Nathan Meyer could be seen pedaling up and down the streets of New York on her bicycle, ringing doorbells and appealing for funds. Her appearance caused a great deal of talk.

Annie did not care. She was probably the very first woman to ride a bicycle in New York, and certainly the first one to single-handedly raise funds for a women's college. She lectured, wrote articles, and negotiated with Columbia University. No amount of disapproval by her family or friends could stop her.

At first, her husband Alfred was one of the few who supported her efforts. Slowly, others joined the cause. In 1899, Annie Nathan Meyer saw her dream come true. Barnard College for Women opened right next door to Columbia University. Annie was thirty-two years old.

Annie Meyer supported Barnard College all her life and served as a trustee. She also became involved in other activities. She addressed the problem of prejudice and urged African-Americans and Jews to take pride in their heritage. She wrote articles, books, and plays.

Despite Annie Meyer's commitment to women's education, she was against giving women the right to vote. Many people who knew her claimed her position was a reaction to her older sister, Maud. The two sisters had competed since they were very young and often fought — when they talked at all.

Maud Nathan Fredericks was a staunch supporter of women's rights. She marched in parades and made speeches at rallies. As forceful and intelligent as Annie, Maud was furious with her sister for her refusal to support a woman's right to vote. To make things worse, Annie joined an anti-women's suffrage group. She said she was worried that uneducated people might use the vote improperly.

When women did win the right to vote in 1920, Annie Nathan Meyer was fifty-three years old. She was still active as a trustee and fund-raiser for Barnard College and was a recognized writer and art critic. Her play, *The Advertising of Kate*, was produced on Broadway in 1921.

Just before her death in 1951, Annie's autobiography, *It's Been Fun*, was published. In it she reveals her family's shocking secrets and the details of her life. *It's Been Fun* also contradicts the book her sister Maud had already written. Maud, who had passed away a few years earlier, could not witness this final outrage.

Annie Nathan Meyer, an independent spirit and a committed activist, continued to astonish her contemporaries until the end of her life.

Annie Nathan Meyer

The West German government made a postage stamp from this photo in 1954. It said: "Bertha Pappenheim, Helper of Humanity."

Chapter 14

Struggling for Change

By the last third of the nineteenth century, in Europe as well as in America, freedom and individual rights were "in the air." Enlightenment was spreading from the large cities of western Europe into the most remote villages of Poland and Russia. Everywhere, people began rebelling against the old ways. Religion itself was being questioned.

Some Jews abandoned Jewish education completely in exchange for the opportunities of the secular universities. Others were convinced that erasing all religious and ethnic differences was necessary to create a better world. Still other Jews became committed to Socialism, a political belief that urged the creation of a classless society. Socialist movements offered active leadership roles for Jewish women who often felt limited by traditional Judaism as it was practiced at that time. It was no longer necessary to convert to Christianity in order to be accepted. Jews could become free thinkers, deists, or even atheists.

Another alternative newly open to Jewish women was the opportunity for leadership within the Jewish community itself. Women as well as men established voluntary organizations to replace the old communal structure, now no longer relevant. They worked to preserve Jewish observance and law and also to raise women's status within Judaism.

Among these new leaders were five women. Each found a different path. Rosa Luxemburg turned away from Judaism, while Sarah Schnirer committed herself to Jewish education for women. Bertha Pappenheim organized a group to promote women's equality in Jewish communal affairs, Lily Montagu helped institute a form of liberal Jewish worship, and Mathilde Schechter worked to find a place for traditional Judaism in American life.

Rosa Luxemburg

Rosa Luxemburg is an example of a Jew who became committed to the new social and political movements of her day. She was born in Warsaw, Poland in 1871. Already partly assimilated, her middle class, merchant parents sent her to a secular school to be educated.

At the age of eleven, Rosa experienced a terrifying pogrom. Violent crowds of Poles roamed the streets of Warsaw. They broke windows, looted, and encouraged each other to beat up Jews. This was Rosa's first contact with anti-Semitism.

As a teenager, she searched for a new and just world where pogroms and hatred of other groups would no longer exist. The Polish Revolutionary Movement offered such a hope, and

Rosa joined while still in high school. She was one of the founders of the Social Democratic Party of Poland and Lithuania and later, of the German Communist Party.

In 1898, after earning a degree in Economics from the University of Zurich, Switzerland, Rosa went to live in Germany. There, she was active as a labor organizer. In 1905 she returned to Warsaw to participate in the Polish Revolution. When that failed, she was captured and imprisoned.

Rosa escaped and returned to Germany, where she continued working with German and Polish laborers in the Socialist International. The International was an organization uniting socialists from all over the world.

Rosa was jailed again when she opposed World War I. Finally, she was murdered by army officers in 1919 while on her way to prison for the third time.

Rosa Luxemburg, an intelligent and well-educated woman, was not exceptional in the choices she made. Many young Jews at that time were flocking to the Socialist movement. She was unique because of her degree of activism and her recognition as a world leader. Although she loved the Yiddish language, she found no meaning in the Jewish religion and eventually came to believe anti-Semitism was not relevant to her or her cause. She never joined the Jewish Labor Movement, which was committed to the preservation of Jewish culture. Instead, she devoted her life to a revolutionary form of socialism, working to make the world a better place for all human beings.

Sarah Schnirer

Unlike Rosa Luxemburg, Sarah Schnirer was committed to Judaism. Born into a Hasidic family in Cracow, Poland, in 1883, she was surrounded by a community of observant Jews. However, the Jewish education she longed for, which was readily available to her father and brothers, was denied her. Along with other Jewish girls her age, she was sent to a Polish public school.

Once her older sister married and left home, Sarah had to spend most of her time helping her mother with household chores. She learned dressmaking and supported herself as a seamstress for a good part of her life.

Although she studied on her own, reading the Bible in Yiddish, and other books written for women, she wanted to learn more. Reluctantly, she turned to the Polish universities that were now open to Jews.

It was common for Orthodox families to neglect their daughters' religious instruction. Fathers assumed that the Jewish rituals the girls needed to know could be learned informally from their mothers.

However, as the Enlightenment spread through the cities of eastern Europe, fewer Jewish women were able to transmit the old traditions. Sarah saw evidence of this while attending a meeting of a local Jewish organization for young women. She realized that most were ignorant of even the basic Jewish rituals. Yet she saw these same young women attending university lectures. They sought knowledge of Polish literature but knew nothing of their own sacred books!

For Sarah, this explained why women were so easily led away from Judaism. She wanted to change these conditions and teach women about their own heritage, but she did not know how.

Then, in 1914, World War I broke out and Sarah Schnirer moved to Vienna with her family. It was in this city that all her ideas and impressions on educating girls came together. In the Stumper Gasse synagogue, Rabbi Dr. Flesch gave a sermon in which he referred to Judith and other Jewish heroines, women who were virtually unknown to most Jews. Begin a study of Judaism, the rabbi implored his listeners.

Sarah Schnirer founded the Beis Yaakov schools for girls.

Sarah later wrote: "I understood instantly that the main problem is that our sisters are alienated from our people and our traditions because they know so little about our past."

Inspired by the sermon, Sarah left the synagogue with a new commitment. She would start a school for girls.

"Throw away your machine," she told herself. "Renounce your trade of sewing clothes for the body, and instead, take up sewing and piecing together clothes for the soul . . . ."

Her new commitment would be challenged from all sides. Some Orthodox Jews insisted that it went against tradition to educate girls. From the Enlightenment side came another reaction: What? In the twentieth century you want to lead Jewish women back to observance of Yiddishkeit (Jewishness)? But Sarah Schnirer would not give up.

Her first attempt at organizing Jewish culture classes for young women was disappointing. Sarah soon realized that she needed to begin with children. A love of Judaism could only be instilled before the girls got older, before they were exposed to the negative ideas about Judaism being taught in the public schools.

With the encouragement of the *Belzer rebbe*, a respected Hassidic leader, Sarah opened a women's library and school in Cracow in 1918. It was called *Beis Yaakov* (the house of Jacob) and consisted of one class of twenty-five girls. Her first students were the children of the customers for whom she had once made dresses.

Sarah's school was greeted with enthusiasm by many Orthodox families and word of its success spread throughout eastern Europe. Appeals to open girls' schools came from all over. "Save our girls," was the cry that went from one community to another.

Schnirer perceived that a school for training teachers was essential to supply the demands of this growing movement. There were soon schools, summer camps, and teachers' seminaries in Cracow, Lodz, and Vienna. Before long, *Beis Yaakov* schools for girls had spread throughout central and eastern Europe as the opposition of Orthodox groups was overcome.

It was always Sarah's goal to work within the traditional Jewish community. For this reason, when the Orthodox Agudath Israel took over the sponsorship of the schools, Sarah willingly stepped down as the administrator. She understood that Orthodox tradition did not approve of women in public life. Instead, she concentrated on writing and on encouraging the use of the Yiddish language among Jews.

Under Agudath Israel, the *Beis Yaakov* schools continued Sarah's goals: to educate girls in Jewish culture, history, law, and tradition and to teach them vocational skills they could use to support themselves.

Sarah Schnirer died in 1935, at the age of fifty-two. By that time, *Beis Yaakov* schools had changed considerably. A single class of twenty-five pupils had grown into a network of over 200 schools with more than 25,000 students. Schnirer's dream of Jewish education for girls had expanded beyond all her expectations. Because of her efforts and accomplishments, a new world of opportunity opened for observant Jewish women.

Bertha Pappenheim

Bertha Pappenheim was also committed to preserving the fabric of Jewish life and to educating women. Her emphasis, however, was different from Sarah Schnirer's.

Born in 1859, the third daughter of a Viennese Orthodox Jewish family, Bertha was immediately a disappointment to her parents, who would have preferred a son. She grew up in a prosperous household, with all the material comforts Vienna could offer. However, her childhood was saddened by the deaths of both her older sisters. A brother, born one and a half years after Bertha, was her only sibling.

Educated in private Catholic schools, Bertha was tutored at home in Jewish religion. As a girl, she was denied the university education given to her brother, a fact she always regretted.

The most critical event in Bertha's life occurred when she was twenty years old. At this time, she nursed her father through a serious illness. Just before he died, she suffered an emotional breakdown and attempted suicide. For a short period of time she was paralyzed and unable to walk or even talk.

Bertha Pappenheim's later accomplishments are even more remarkable when we consider these early problems. Bertha regained her health partly through the aid of Dr. Joseph Breuer, a famous Viennese

Bertha Pappenheim

physician and a friend of Sigmund Freud. Freud, a Viennese Jewish doctor, developed a method for treating mental illness based on his theory of the unconscious mind.

Breuer treated Bertha for a period of eighteen months with this new method that she called "the talking cure." It was later called *psychoanalysis*. Together, Freud and Breuer wrote about Bertha's case. In order to protect her privacy, they referred to her as "Anna O." *The Case of Anna O* became famous in the field of psychology and psychoanalysis.

Even after her worst symptoms went away, Bertha spent several years recuperating, and for a while was sent to a sanitarium. No records remain of this time in her life. Six years after her illness, Pappenheim, at least partially recovered, moved to Frankfurt with her mother. There she joined other female members of her family who were involved in Jewish communal work.

By throwing herself into social work and women's activities, Bertha overcame her depression and physical weakness. She never spoke about her illness and devoted the rest of her years to German Jewish girls and women, their needs and education.

In the mid-nineteenth century, many people believed that women were more spiritual and moral than men. The new theories about women claimed that their higher morality meant they were better able to help others. But women were still ignored in the male-dominated social service agencies that were being established by Jews.

In 1902, Pappenheim decided to form a modern social welfare organization for women. She called it Women's Welfare. Bertha taught the women workers about child care and introduced new techniques for recording the case histories of their clients. The women at Women's Welfare set up a day care center with employment services especially for women.

Bertha also wanted to help women obtain social, political, and economic rights in Germany and within the Jewish community. With these goals in mind, Pappenheim founded *Die Juedischer Frauenbund* (The League of Jewish Women) in 1904.

As president of the *Frauenbund*, Bertha edited its newsletter, made speeches, led study groups, and taught the principles of social work to others. She also wrote and translated Yiddish works into German. Among them was the *Memoir of Gluckel of Hameln*. Bertha was a direct descendant of Gluckel.

Pappenheim was also committed to stopping the forced prostitution of poor women and girls, a practice known as "white slavery." When she came up against the indifference of the established Jewish community, Bertha insisted: "Nobody is allowed to remain quiet if he knows that something wrong is being done." Pappenheim set up homes for these prostitutes and their children, many of whom were Jewish. This work gave her great satisfaction.

Bertha Pappenheim, who never married, died on the eve of World War II, soon after being questioned by the Gestapo, the Nazi Police. She was seventy-seven years old. In 1954 the West German government honored her by putting her picture on a postage stamp with the words "Bertha Pappenheim, Helper of Humanity."

Lily Montagu

Lily Montagu, a London Jew, addressed herself to the same problems as her sisters in Germany and Poland: assimilation of Jews and lack of education for Jewish women.

Born in 1873 into a large and prosperous Jewish family, Lilian Helen was the sixth child of Samuel and Ellen Montagu. She and her younger sister Marian were sent to a public school and were tutored at home in Jewish subjects. Their teacher of Judaism, Simeon Singer of the New West End synagogue, taught Lily to appreciate her religious tradition.

Lily's first involvement with Jewish communal life began at the age of seventeen, when Singer suggested she conduct a children's service at the synagogue. To hold the interest of the young people, Lily developed a simple order of prayers in English, and gave informal talks. The services soon became so successful that many women attended together with their children.

Neither Lily nor her sister Marian ever married. Lily's work was her life. Her family was very wealthy and she had no concerns about money.

Lily Montagu's first venture beyond her own family and community was her involvement in the education of Jewish working girls. Like her children's services, this project was a success.

Lily Montagu founded Liberal Judaism in England.

The young working women who attended Lily's classes soon developed into a permanent group: The West Central Club for Jewish working girls. Classes and services expanded over five years to include social activities as well.

During those years Lily's personal religious convictions gradually took shape. Lily saw God as the source of goodness, love, and truth, and emphasized individual faith and high moral standards rather than ritual. To work for these changes, Lily Montagu established the Jewish Religious Union (JRU) in 1902, and became one of its vice-presidents. Lily had hoped the JRU would work for change within traditional Judaism. Instead, it became an alternative to Orthodoxy and sponsored the first Liberal Jewish Synagogue in 1911. Liberal Judaism was the English counterpart to Germany's Reform Movement. It soon expanded to several branches and formed the Union of Liberal Jewish Organizations, an international group of Reform Congregations. In 1928, Lily Montagu was invited to preach at the Union's second meeting in Berlin. She had been the first woman to preach sermons in a synagogue in England. Now she also became the first woman to speak from the pulpit in a German synagogue.

In her speech, Lily did not discuss issues of women's equality. She stressed the importance of individual faith, and the need for personal and organized religion to work together.

Montagu gained recognition in the Jewish and secular world as a social worker. She was a religious organizer, a writer of novels, essays and prayers, a magistrate in London's juvenile courts, and a spiritual leader. She worked to gain the vote for women and to include them equally in Jewish life.

In 1938, Lily Montagu was unanimously acclaimed the new president of the JRU, a post she held until 1945. In 1963, after her death at the age of ninety, the JRU building was named in her honor: The Lily Montagu Center of Living Judaism.

During her long life, Montagu forged a role of activism and equality. She paved the way for other Jewish women to participate fully in religious life.

Mathilde Roth Schechter

Mathilde Roth, the youngest child in a large family, was born in Guttentag, Silesia (a part of present-day Germany) on December 16, 1859. There is no information about her mother, but her father, a wheat merchant, died suddenly when she was still very young. Mathilde was brought up by her older brother and educated first at a Jewish orphan home and then at a municipal high school. Her exceptional intelligence made her an excellent candidate for advanced studies, and she graduated from a teacher's seminary in Germany.

Mathilde's first assignment was in Hungary but she soon managed to find a private teaching position in England. In 1885, she arrived in London and settled in with the Friedlanders as tutor to their daughter. Dr. Michael Friedlander was the principal of Jews' College and it was in the Jews' College Library that Mathilde met Dr. Solomon Schechter, a scholar and tutor to Claude Montefiore. The two were married in June 1887.

Within a few years of their marriage, Mathilde gave birth to three children: Ruth, Frank, and Amy. To help earn money for the family, she organized classes for women in German literature and art history and also tutored private students. She enjoyed an active role as hostess to her husband's colleagues, both in London and then at Cambridge, where Solomon got his first academic appointment in 1890.

It was in Cambridge that the Cairo Geniza was brought to Solomon Schechter's attention and he traveled to Egypt to examine the documents (see Chapter 4). Mathilde also continued her intellectual pursuits. Although never published, she translated Heinrich Heine's poems into English and the work of her friend Israel Zangwill into German.

Solomon Schechter's reputation as a scholar grew. In 1902 he was invited to head the Jewish Theological Seminary of America, the major educational school for Conservative

Judaism in the United States. Mathilde and Solomon, together with their children, journeyed to New York City to begin a new life.

In New York Mathilde founded the Columbia Street Religious and Technical School for Jewish Girls where she taught Jewish culture for several years. The school was a milestone in American Jewish life, where few Jewish religious schools accepted girls. She also embraced Zionism and was one of the early supporters of Hadassah, founded in 1912 by Henrietta Szold (see Chapter 15).

The Schechter home was known for its warmth and hospitality. Mathilde's role was comparable to that of the eighteenth-century salon women of Germany (see Chapter 12). The important difference was that Mathilde Schechter presided over a salon of *Jewish* intellectuals, and remained dedicated to Judaism. During these informal discussions in her living room, she gained the reputation of a woman with considerable knowledge of Jewish literature.

Mathilde Schechter, founder of the National Women's League for Conservative Judaism.

Rumors at the Seminary that she had "ghost written" many of her husband's essays from his notes were never proven. Scholars point to Solomon's poor English grammar when he wrote to Mathilde and the excellent English of his articles and books, all of which were typed and edited by his wife.

When Schechter founded the United Synagogue of America in 1913, the new organization was meant to include lay people, not just rabbis. All would work together in the cause of Conservative Judaism, including women. Mathilde and Solomon conceived of women's work as a perpetuation of traditional Judaism in the homes, synagogues, and communities of American Jews.

Two years after the establishment of United Synagogue, Solomon Schechter died. Mathilde continued their shared vision. Within three years, she persuaded faculty wives and prominent community leaders to join her in organizing the National Women's League for Conservative Judaism. Mathilde Schechter was its first president. She created programs and publications which became models for the future.

Mathilde Roth Schechter died in 1924, but she remains an example of how married Jewish women, while devoted to home and family, can make substantial contributions to Jewish life.

Golda Meir left America to settle in Palestine.

Chapter 15

The Call of the Jewish Homeland

Many significant ideas and goals competed for the attention of Jews at the turn of the twentieth century. Jewish education, social services, modernized religious practices, and the fight for equal opportunity all had their supporters among Jews. But another concept transformed Judaism and Jewish life more than any other. That was Zionism.

Zionism — the belief that Jews are a people entitled to a land of their own — was an old idea. Jews had believed this ever since they were driven out of the land of Israel by the Romans from 68 to 70 C.E.

Through the long centuries of exile, Jews never forgot the Holy Land and small numbers never left. After the Jews were expelled from Spain and Portugal in 1492, Gracia Nasi sponsored a Jewish settlement in Galilee. Judith and Moses Montefiore gave large sums of money to help the Jews of Palestine become self-supporting.

However, the Jews in the Holy Land remained poor. Under Turkish rule, the region was economically depressed and there were few jobs available. The Montefiore's attempt to bring agriculture to the Jews of the area was only partly successful. Jews survived on charitable contributions from abroad and had little influence on the Jewish communities of the West.

The new Zionist movement changed all that. Beginning with a handful of Zionist philosophers from Eastern Europe, modern Zionism built on the traditional concept of a "return to Zion," but added new ideas.

One relatively new idea spreading throughout Europe was political nationalism. Small city-states were combining into nations. Ethnic groups were organizing themselves into modern states. Why not the Jews?

The interest in Jewish culture and education also became a factor in the new Zionism. Education had been the focus of so many of Europe's Jews. The Zionists went one step further. They claimed that Jews could freely enjoy their own culture, language, and religion only in a Jewish state.

A third factor that influenced the Zionist movement was anti-Semitism. In spite of their growing assimilation, Jews continued to be viewed by many gentiles as different, dangerous, and unwanted. Theodore Herzl, a principal spokesperson for modern political Zionism, offered a solution to that problem. He claimed that the only way anti-Semitism could be eliminated was for the Jews to leave Europe and create a Jewish homeland.

Encouraged by these ideas, and excited by the political pamphlets and speeches of the new Zionist thinkers, hundreds of young Jews joined the movement. They set up training centers in Russia and Poland where they could learn about farming. They prepared themselves for *aliyah* (immigration) to *Eretz Israel* (the land of Israel).

After arriving in Palestine, Jews confronted rugged conditions and long days of hard labor; they also faced Arab hostility. The Arabs resented Jews from Europe for buying land and changing the area. Arab residents had made a living for centuries as nomadic shepherds. By draining swamps, modernizing agriculture, and building cities and roads throughout the desert, the Jews threatened the traditional Arab way of life.

Women Pioneers preparing a vegetable garden in Palestine, 1920.

Partly because of these difficult and dangerous conditions, most of the settlers who went on the first or second *aliyah* were men, but there were some young women among them. These heroic pioneers left comfortable middle class homes in Europe and America to live in conditions of extreme hardship. Some died of malaria and other diseases. Some were killed by hostile Arabs.

Sarah Malchin

The first woman to arrive in *Eretz Israel* as part of the early Zionist immigration was Sarah Malchin. She came in 1901, while still in her late teens, the only woman in a group of men. All had received some agricultural training in Russia before they left.

This working group (*kvutzah* was the word in Hebrew) settled in the

Kinneret, an area in the north of Palestine. While the men worked the land, Sarah was assigned to the kitchen. It was assumed that this was "women's work" and not appropriate for men.

Although she was disappointed at not being able to work the fields, Sarah made the best of her situation. She had no experience in running a household, and certainly not in dealing with the primitive conditions that existed in Palestine in the 1900s. Nevertheless, she single-handedly managed the kitchen, did the laundry, and nursed the workers when they were sick.

The men grew to depend on her. However, when Sarah begged to be able to recruit more women so she could be relieved of some of her duties, they refused. Disappointed, she left and joined a new training farm for girls. This farm was organized in 1911 by Hannah Meisel, another young woman pioneer from eastern Europe.

Unfortunately, Sarah's difficult life of hard work and inadequate food made her ill. Since there were no medical facilities in Palestine, she was forced to return to Vienna. A friend who had known her in Palestine, commented sadly on her appearance:

"When I met her in the Kinneret she was healthy, pretty and blooming . . . After some years had passed, I met her in the hospital in Vienna and I didn't recognize her."

In spite of her illness, Sarah insisted on returning to the hard life of Palestine. She was one of the founders of *Degania*, Israel's first collective agricultural settlement (kibbutz).

By the time of her death in 1949, Sarah Malchin had become a heroine for other women immigrating to *Eretz Israel*. Like Sarah, many of these young pioneers struggled not only for the Zionist dream, but also for the right to work — or fight — as equals with men.

Sarah Chizick

Sarah Chizick, born in 1897, was one of the first women to die defending a Jewish settlement in Palestine.

Sarah's Russian parents were committed Zionists. In 1908, when Sarah was eleven, her entire family immigrated to Palestine. Like most of the early Zionist pioneers, Sarah was determined to work the land and make the deserts of the new Jewish state bloom.

Sarah loved nature. She spent much of her spare time gathering and naming the wild flowers of the country. Her collection was later donated to one of the museums in Jerusalem.

As Hannah Meisel had done a few years earlier, Sarah and her sister Hannah Chizick organized a farm school for girls. To support themselves, the young women raised vegetables which they sold to the German soldiers stationed in Palestine during World War I (1914–1918).

Sarah wanted to do even more for her homeland. In 1920 a call came for volunteers to travel to the settlement of Tel Hai, far to the north of Haifa, and defend it from Arab attacks. Sarah and her friend Deborah Drachler came forward. They were the only women among forty men.

Neither the leader of the group, Joseph Trumpeldor, nor the other volunteers wanted these two women to join them. Sarah and Deborah were insistent. They marched with the men all night. The terrain was so rocky that it cut their shoes and made their feet bloody.

Arriving at Tel Hai at dawn, they were caught in a surprise attack. Sarah and Deborah, as well as commander Joseph Trumpeldor, were among the eight volunteers who were killed. A monument to these brave young people stands on the spot. The inscription reads: "It is good to die for our country."

Manya Shochat

Manya Wilbushewitch Shochat was one of the most revolutionary of the Jewish women of twentieth-century eastern Europe. Born in Grodno, Russia in 1880, she was one of many children in the Wilbushewitch family. Her parents were wealthy and assimilated and the children received a secular as well as a Jewish education.

Always a rebel, Manya left home at the age of fifteen to become a worker in Minsk. She soon was part of a revolutionary circle and by the time she was twenty had already been arrested by the Russian secret police for her political activities.

During Manya's time in prison she was questioned by a man named Zubatov, head of Moscow's Secret Police. He persuaded Manya to organize a non-political workers movement when she was released from prison. This type of organization was more acceptable to the tzarist regime. It concentrated on improving the economic conditions of the workers rather than political revolution.

Once freed, Manya did help found the Jewish Labor Party, which functioned from 1901 until 1903. That year, word of the devastating pogrom at Kishinev began to spread among the Jewish population.

The attack at Kishinev was preceded by a campaign of anti-Semitism, planned and carried out by Russian officials with the help of the local police chief. Forty-nine Jews were killed and 500 injured at Kishinev. After two days of looting and rioting, 2,000 Jews were left homeless. This shocking event prompted a major emigration of Jews out of Russia.

Manya was horrified by the suffering of her people. She became involved in a plot to assassinate Russia's Minister of the Interior, a known anti-Semite. When she learned that her co-

conspirators had been arrested, some even killed, she was deeply depressed. It seemed that her revolutionary work accomplished nothing.

At this crossroad in her life, Manya received a letter from Palestine where her brother Nahum was living. He urged her to join him there and she agreed. In early 1904, Manya arrived in *Eretz Israel* and traveled throughout the land. She visited the struggling agricultural settlements and formed a plan.

The only way for Jewish farm workers to succeed, she insisted, was to organize collective settlements. Each member would contribute to a common effort, and all would receive an equal share of the proceeds. Manya's plan was destined to become the model for the kibbutz movement in Israel.

In 1905 Manya left Palestine to raise funds for a new settlement that would put her ideas into practice. While in Paris, a friend pleaded with her to smuggle weapons into Russia. Arms and ammunition would enable Russian Jews to protect themselves from pogroms.

Manya consented, but on her arrival in Odessa with trunks of weapons, things began to go wrong. She discovered that the "safe house" in which she was staying was being watched by the secret police. The smuggled arms could not be moved.

While she was waiting for further instructions, a young man came to the house claiming to be a friend of the absent tenants. Following a conversation with him, Manya began to suspect that he was a tzarist spy. She supposedly waited until the police left the area and then shot and killed him.

There were no immediate consequences for Manya after this incident. However, years later, suspicion would fall on her for this murder, which many of her associates considered a rash act.

Back in *Eretz Israel* by the end of 1907, Manya joined *Bar Giora*. This group was named for a Jewish military leader who had been active in the war against Rome from 66 to 70 C.E. *Bar Giora* was led by Israel Shochat. Israel and Manya, along with other members of *Bar Giora*, went north to the Galilee and settled in a training farm village called Sejera. There, in 1907, they founded the forerunner of the first agricultural collective (kibbutz) of the new homeland. One year later, Manya Wilbushewitch and Israel Shochat were married.

In 1909, Manya and Israel founded *HaShomer*, an organization of armed guards. *Shomrim* (the Hebrew word for guards) were essential to protect the small Jewish settlements from Arab attacks. Dressed in Bedouin clothing, a rifle on her shoulder, Manya also took her turn to ride out on horseback and defend the settlement. *HaShomer* later became the basis for the modern Israeli Army.

Many who came to Sejera became the great builders and leaders of Israel. David Ben

Gurion, Israel's first prime minister, began his pioneering work there. Izhak Ben-Zvi, Israel's second president, and his future wife Rachel Yanait were also part of Sejera.

During World War I, Manya and Israel Shochat were exiled from Palestine by the Turkish authorities, who accused them of helping the British. For several years they lived in Turkey. When the British took over Palestine, the Shochats returned.

Shortly before the war's end, on November 2, 1917, the foreign secretary of England, Arthur James Balfour, wrote a letter that would affect Jews all over the world. Addressed to Lord Walter Rothschild, a wealthy Jew who was the symbolic head of England's Jewish community, the letter read: "His Majesty's government view with favor the establishment in Palestine of a national home for the Jewish people."

With British support for a Jewish homeland, and the end of the war, Jewish immigration increased. New settlements and organizations

Manya Shochat

was among the most

radical of

the early Zionist

pioneers.

were created. Manya became a founding member of Histadrut, the Jewish Labor Union, in 1921. She and her husband Israel were part of the group now guiding the Jewish State toward independence.

However, Manya's involvement with the murder in Odessa came back to haunt her. The British may have learned about this past crime from an informer. They arrested her as a suspect after the violent death of a Jewish spy in Palestine.

Although Manya was soon released, the arrest created a rift between her and Ben Gurion. Old charges of her involvement with Zubatov, once head of the Russian secret police, also surfaced. Many Russian Jewish revolutionaries had been suspicious of Zubatov. Their misgivings were confirmed when he was disgraced by the tzarist government and committed suicide. Associates who remembered Manya's commitment to Zubatov's goals began to question her judgment and loyalty.

From the late 1920s, Manya Shochat faced one disappointment after another. In spite of her hard work and her status as a founder, women were refused equal membership in *HaShomer*. They were also squeezed out of important positions in other organizations.

In 1930, Manya attempted to found the League for Jewish Arab Coexistence. Hoping to create a spirit of cooperation between Arabs and Jews, she appealed to many of her friends, including David Ben Gurion. There was little response.

In her personal life there were frustrations as well. Israel Shochat was an unfaithful husband and their marriage was unhappy. Her children resented her frequent absences. All her energies had been devoted to her revolutionary and Zionist activities at the expense of her family.

When the state of Israel was established in 1948, Manya Shochat was not given a post in the new government. But her commitment never wavered. She joined Israel's socialist party, and worked with Holocaust survivors in transit and labor camps.

Years after Manya's death in 1961, Rachel Yanait Ben-Zvi wrote a biography of her old friend. Entitled *Before Golda: Manya Shochat*, the book recognized Manya's important contributions to the independent state of Israel.

Henrietta Szold

Henrietta Szold was born in the United States in 1860. She never experienced a pogrom nor saw much anti-Semitism. As a young girl she did not dream of life in a Jewish homeland. Yet she contributed more to the state of Israel than many who did.

The oldest of five daughters, Henrietta grew up surrounded by Jewish learning and tradition. Her father was a rabbi in Baltimore, and, by the time Henrietta was in her teens, she was helping him translate and edit his sermons, books, and letters.

Henrietta also shared her father's concern for the Russian Jewish immigrants, newly arrived in Baltimore. These Jews were part of a major migration of Russian Jews to America in the late 1800s, which was prompted by Russia's anti-Jewish policies. Some of the immigrants settled in Baltimore where a small Jewish community already existed. Henrietta helped them to set up a night school. She taught classes and acted as the supervising principal.

All this work developed Henrietta's writing skills and deepened her knowledge of Judaism. Before long, she was invited to serve as secretary, then as editor for the Jewish Publication Society in Philadelphia. As editor, Henrietta supervised the publication of many important Jewish books and translated others. She worked for The Jewish Publication Society on and off for eighteen years.

It was not until the late 1890s, as a result of her involvement with Russian Jews, that Henrietta became interested in Zionism. She read the works of Leo Pinsker and Theodore Herzl. These philosophers were convinced that Jews had to create a homeland in Palestine for themselves.

In a speech before the Baltimore chapter of the National Council of Jewish Women in 1896, Henrietta publicly supported the Zionist cause for the first time. A few years later, at the age of forty, she became a member of the executive committee of the Federation of American Zionists.

Then in 1902, Rabbi Szold, Henrietta's father, died. He had been her teacher, friend, and confidant for so many years that his passing left an empty space in her life. When her mother suggested that Henrietta prepare his papers for publication, she agreed. However, she felt she needed more background in Talmud and rabbinics. In order to gain that knowledge, Henrietta applied to The Jewish Theological Seminary in New York.

No women had yet studied at the new Conservative seminary for rabbis, but Henrietta was allowed to attend classes with the understanding that she would not apply for the rabbinate. It was at the seminary that Henrietta first met Louis Ginzberg, a young scholar from Lithuania who was teaching classes in Talmud. A friendship soon developed between them.

Before long, Henrietta was helping Ginzberg with his English and translating and editing his work. The two became close, spending hours together, discussing ideas and preparing Ginzberg's massive manuscript, *Legends of the Jews.*

Henrietta realized she had fallen in love with Louis. She was forty-three years old, and Louis Ginzberg was thirty years old. He had never spoken to her about love and marriage. Yet, somehow, Henrietta deceived herself into believing that she and Louis could build a life together.

Henrietta never told Louis she loved him. In 1908, Ginzberg decided to marry and traveled to Europe to find a wife. His bride was Adele Katzenstein, a pretty young German Jewish woman, twenty-two years old.

Henrietta was shocked and devastated. Seemingly oblivious to her hurt, Louis expected them to continue working as before. Tortured by doubts, Henrietta even thought about suicide. She had spent her forty-three years doing other people's work. Now she had nothing for herself.

It was time to change her life. When Henrietta's mother proposed a trip abroad, Henrietta agreed. She could rest, forget, and also visit Palestine where Zionists were building a homeland.

On that first trip, Henrietta saw poverty and disease everywhere. There was little or no medical care.

"This is what your Hadassah Study Circle should do," Henrietta's mother suggested. She was referring to the woman's Zionist study group to which Henrietta belonged. Instead of just learning

Zionist philosophy, why not organize medical and nursing units for Palestine?

Henrietta quickly acted on this idea. By 1912, a constitution had been drawn up for the new organization, with Szold at the head. Its goals were "the promotion of Jewish institutions and enterprises in Palestine and the fostering of Jewish ideals." The group was called Hadassah, after Queen Esther whose Hebrew name was Hadassah.

Hadassah's first objective was to send two nurses to Jerusalem to care for the sick, followed by a medical team. However, World War I intervened and Turkey prevented any medical aid from reaching Palestine from America.

The end of the war and the publication of the Balfour Declaration led to

Henrietta Szold, founder of Hadassah and Youth Aliyah and the first editor of The Jewish Publication Society.

many improvements. Medical supplies, doctors, and nurses flowed into Palestine. Hadassah was established as the women's auxiliary to the American Zionists. Henrietta began receiving a regular stipend from wealthy American Zionists so she could devote herself to public health in Palestine.

In 1920, Henrietta Szold moved to the developing Jewish homeland. Although she took many trips to America and Europe, Jerusalem remained her home from that time until her death.

Despite many problems, a nursing school graduated its first class of trained nurses in 1921. A team of doctors and nurses worked throughout Palestine, setting up hospitals, clinics, and laboratories in major cities. A pasteurized milk station distributed safe milk for children, and newly trained midwives delivered babies. Henrietta quickly learned the business of medicine and the needs of each project. Then in 1933 a new challenge came from Europe.

The aftermath of World War I had brought increasing poverty and anti-Semitism to Germany, and Jewish youth had little future there. A German Jewish woman named Recha Freier conceived of the idea of sending young German Jews to Palestine to work the land. Henrietta Szold, now an honorary juvenile probation officer under the British Mandate, was contacted to help with the plan.

At first Henrietta was doubtful whether this was a good idea. Life was hard on the settlements and these young people would be far from their families. Despite her reservations, though, she went to gather the first group of children.

The *aliyah* of German youth proved successful. With the rise of Hitler and Nazism, more children

Henrietta Szold in 1921 with the first class of graduating nurses in Israel.

were sent with Youth Aliyah to Palestine. Henrietta Szold became a mother to these Jewish youngsters. In Haifa, she personally greeted each boatload of children and supervised their assignment to kibbutzim and youth villages. Finally, the outbreak of World War II put an end to the rescue effort.

Henrietta Szold died in 1945 at the age of eighty-five. She did not live to see Israel become an independent state. However, her contributions live on throughout the Jewish homeland. Her legacy includes Hadassah's hospital and nursing school, a social welfare system, and Youth Aliyah villages.

Golda Meir

Like so many other Zionists, Golda Mabovitch experienced the terror of pogroms. Born in Russia in 1898, one of her earliest memories was watching her father board up their house to protect the family against anti-

Semitic attacks.

By the time Golda was eight years old, her family emigrated to the United States and settled in Milwaukee, Wisconsin. Her father, Moshe, worked as a carpenter and her mother opened a small store. Golda and her two sisters began school in Milwaukee.

When Golda became a teenager, she and her parents began to clash. Golda's mother, Bluma, urged her daughter to marry. At the age of fourteen or fifteen, Golda was not ready for marriage. She wanted to study and become a teacher, but her parents disapproved of higher education for women.

The tension between Golda and her mother became worse until finally Golda ran away to live with her sister Shana. Shana, nine years older than Golda, was married and living in Denver, Colorado. In Denver, Golda was deeply impressed with the Zionists who gathered in her sister's home. She began raising money for Zionist causes and talked about living in *Eretz Israel*. Although she had come to Denver to avoid marriage, it was there that she met her future husband, Morris Meyerson.

Only fifteen years old, Golda thought she loved Morris, but she was determined to live her life in a Jewish homeland. Morris had fled from Russia to the safety of America where he wanted to remain.

After a year in Denver, Golda returned to Milwaukee. Her parents promised there would be no more talk of marriage. Golda finished high school, joined the Labor Zionist movement, and prepared to go to a school for teachers. She and Morris saw each other, but Golda was still determined to go to *Eretz Israel*.

Late in 1917, World War I was almost over when Golda learned of the Balfour Declaration granting the Jews a homeland. She could hardly wait to leave for Palestine. Morris, not wanting to lose his beloved Golda, finally agreed to go with her. Three years later, with enough money saved, they married and left for Palestine.

Golda and Morris Meyerson joined *Merhavia*, a collective settlement (kibbutz) in the Galilee. Golda adapted to kibbutz life, but Morris was not happy, so the couple moved to Jerusalem where Morris found an office job.

For the next few years Golda was a traditional housewife, staying at home with her son and daughter, but now *she* was unhappy. She accepted an offer from Histadrut, the Jewish Labor organization, to work with the Women's Labor Council. In spite of Morris' opposition, she set her foot on the path that she would follow for the rest of her life. Eventually it led to the breakup of her marriage.

Although Golda regretted leaving her children at home, she felt that the developing Jewish state needed her talents. In 1932 she toured the United States for two years, speaking to American Jewish women, raising enthusiasm and money. When she returned home, she was invited to join the Executive Committee of Histadrut.

On the eve of World War II, many Jews were trying to escape from Hitler and Nazi Germany to the relative safety of Palestine. This increased immigration made the Arab residents feel more threatened than ever. They did not want a Jewish homeland and pressured the English government, still in control in the Middle East, to keep Jews out. England agreed and closed Palestine's doors to the desperate Jewish refugees.

Throughout these critical years, Golda was one of the chief negotiators with England. She tried her best to convince the British to allow Jewish immigration to Palestine. A more open immigration policy would have helped save many Jews from death in the Holocaust. Although Golda was not successful in these negotiations, she rose steadily in the ranks of the provisional government of Palestine. As the proclamation declaring Jewish independence neared, Golda was sent on a dangerous mission.

One of several stamps

of Golda Meir

issued by the Israeli

government.

Disguised as an Arab woman, she was smuggled across the border into Jordan. She tried to persuade King Abdullah to keep his promise not to attack the new state. Abdullah of Jordan refused, saying he could not oppose his Arab allies.

Four days later, on May 14, 1948, Israel declared itself an independent nation. Golda Meyerson was one of the two women who signed that declaration. With tears running freely down her cheeks, she took the pen that was handed to her and wrote her name.

Israel was immediately recognized by the United States and the Soviet Union. The new prime minister, David Ben Gurion, opened the borders, and Jews from over seventy different lands poured in. At the same time, Israel was attacked by seven Arab countries and was forced to fight for its existence. The War of Independence lasted a full year and ended with an armistice but no peace.

In the new state of Israel, Golda was appointed minister to Moscow from 1948 to 1949. On her return she became Minister of Labor and Development and had to cope with the large number of refugees who needed homes, work, medical care, food, and clothing.

In 1956, Golda became Foreign Minister, the second highest post in the government. At the request of Ben Gurion, Golda Mabovitch Meyerson changed her name to Golda Meir, a name that reflected the Hebrew language.

In 1969, at the age of seventy-one, Golda Meir was selected as prime minister of Israel. She was the first woman to hold that post, and one of the few women in the world who were prominent in government.

The greatest crisis of Prime Minister Meir's rule came when Israel was attacked in October, 1973. During the Yom Kippur holiday, the Egyptian army crossed the border. At the same time, Syrian troops invaded from the north. The Israeli forces, caught unprepared, sustained heavy losses.

Meir took full responsibility for not having the Israeli troops ready for war. "I shall live with that terrible knowledge for the rest of my life," she later wrote.

After a month of bitter fighting, Israel finally managed to drive back both the Egyptians and the Syrians and a cease-fire was arranged. By that time, Golda Meir had retired. She was seventy-five years old. She died on December 8, 1978, after a struggle with leukemia.

Golda Meir shared the leadership of Israel through countless government crises, terrorist massacres, and bloody wars. She lived to see thirty years of Israeli independence and glimpsed the beginning of peace with Egypt. More than she had ever dreamed as a girl, Golda had helped to build a Jewish homeland.

Lillian Wald founded the Visiting Nurse Service of New York City.

Chapter 16

Working for a Better Life

Anti-Semitism, combined with poverty and pogroms, drove thousands of Jews out of Russia and Poland. Some settled in what would become the state of Israel. Many more came to the United States, known to millions of Europeans as the "golden land."

Once they arrived in American cities, Jewish immigrants found that the "golden land" was not as perfect as they had hoped. They lived in crowded, dirty rooms and worked hard for little pay. Sometimes everyone in a family, even the youngest children, had to work so there would be enough money for food.

A large percentage of Jewish workers, especially single women, found jobs in the garment industry. Married women often added to the meager family income by doing piecework at home and taking in boarders. Those who worked in factories faced twelve hour work days in unsafe and crowded conditions. It was not long before the newcomers realized that if they wanted to improve their working conditions, they would have to organize.

The earliest labor unions were for men only and included mostly skilled laborers. Unions that organized unskilled labor often barred women, seeing them as competition for the same jobs at lower pay. Women soon understood that they would have to take care of themselves.

Despite the violent opposition of bosses and factory owners — and sometimes of the government itself — women workers met together, founded unions, and marched out on strike. Although women organizers and strikers came from all ethnic groups, at least one quarter of them were Jewish. Many were already committed to socialism and working class rights before coming to America. Others became more radical as a result of conditions in their new country.

Although Russian Jewish immigrant women were in the forefront of the effort to improve working conditions, they were not its only heroines. Middle class Jewish women, many from comfortable homes who did not have to work, also committed their lives to these causes. Leaving the confines of their homes, they expanded their domestic world by joining with other women in clubs and organizations. The goal of many of these groups was to reform society. They assisted the poor, worked to end child labor, and helped organize unions in the United States.

Clara Lemlich Shevelson

It took a great deal of courage for a laborer to agree to strike in the early 1900s. Sometimes the few pennies she earned each day were the only money she had to feed herself and her children. Nevertheless, thousands of people, Jews and gentiles, took the risk and banded together. Some did not yet speak English when they joined the picket lines, demanding better working conditions.

Clara Lemlich rallied workers to the first general strike in New York City.

One such worker was Clara Lemlich, a Jewish immigrant from eastern Europe. Clara was a garment worker in a New York City factory. While still in her teens she was already a member of the executive committee of her union. She was arrested seventeen times for protesting. Beaten by strike breakers while marching on the picket line, Clara summoned enough strength to encourage her friends: "Stand fast, girls!" she shouted, as she was dragged off to jail.

On November 22, 1909, Clara was released from the hospital where she had been treated for six broken ribs. Despite this injury, she attended a meeting of all workers in the garment trades. Its purpose was to decide whether or not to declare a general strike.

Crammed in with thousands of other workers, Clara listened to one male speaker after another. They spoke for hours but seemed to be saying very little. Finally, exasperated at the lack of leadership, Clara asked to speak. From the platform this "wisp of a girl," as she was described afterwards, shouted to the crowd:

I am a working girl, one of those who are on strike against intolerable conditions. I am tired of listening to speakers talk in general terms. What we are here for is to decide whether we shall or shall not strike. I offer a resolution that a general strike be declared — now.

Clara spoke in Yiddish, but at least sixty percent of the garment workers were Jewish and they understood her plea. The audience began to cheer wildly. They took an oath to support each other no matter what would happen. So began the first general strike in New York City, started by a young Yiddish-speaking woman.

Although it meant abandoning her plans for an education, Clara remained loyal to the strikers. She was active in the labor union movement for most of her life, even after she was married and stopped working at a paying job.

As a member of the Consumers' League, Clara campaigned against child labor. She also took a leadership role in the Women's Trade Union League. This organization assisted working women, offered support to women strikers, and raised bail money. Through the Women's Trade Union League Clara worked for women's suffrage (right to vote) and helped forge an alliance between working class and middle class women.

Clara Lemlich Shevelson died in 1982, in her nineties. Although few remember her contribution to American labor, her name lives on in histories and union records as a pioneer and supporter of working women's rights.

Rose Schneiderman

Rose Schneiderman was born in Russia in 1882 and emigrated to New York with her family when she was eight years old. Two years later, Rose's father died. Forced to work in a factory, her mother did the only thing she could. She sent her children to an orphanage.

When Rose was thirteen, she was considered old enough to work. Now the younger children were able to stay home with their mother and the family was reunited.

The first job Rose held was errand girl in a department store. She worked sixty-four hours a week and received a weekly wage of $2.16. Her second job, in a more fashionable store, paid $2.75 per week.

Rose soon learned that factory work, although difficult, paid more money. With the help of a friend she found a job as an apprentice in a woman's cap factory. By 1903, Rose had organized the first female local within the United Hat and Cap Makers Union. In a short time, she was on the executive board of the general union, the first woman to hold such a high position.

Rose Schneiderman was an active organizer. After Clara Lemlich's speech ignited the first general strike in New York City, Schneiderman helped organize the women in Clara's factory. She also enlisted women to mount a general strike in the White Goods Workers Union in 1913. In 1914, she was one of the founders of the International Ladies Garment Workers Union.

Having grown up in the factories, Rose knew how bad conditions were, especially for

Rose Schneiderman

devoted her life to

working women and

the labor movement.

young women. Factory owners charged each worker for the supplies she used in her work. Workers had to pay for thread, machines, even electricity. Sometimes the women were expected to scrub the floor at the end of the week before they received their checks, while the men were paid first and went home.

Rose fought against all these policies. In speeches to raise money for striking workers, she tried to educate the middle class about the difficult and unfair conditions.

Sexual harassment was very common at that time and Rose was one of the few union leaders who tried to combat it. She often spoke to factory foremen, condemning them for pinching the girls while they worked, or withholding their pay in hopes of obtaining sexual favors.

Unsafe conditions were also a major problem for workers, especially women. Women were often locked in so they would not be able to strike, or even leave the factory, without permission.

One consequence of this policy was the tragic fire in the Triangle Shirt Waist Company which occurred on March 25, 1911. Over one hundred and forty women were burned to death, many because they were not able to get out of the building. A few days later, Rose Schneiderman spoke at a memorial for the dead workers. She was bitter and resentful.

"This is not the first time girls have been burned alive," she said. "Every year thousands of us are maimed. The life of men and women is so cheap, and property is so sacred. There are so many of us for one job it matters little if a hundred forty-three of us are burned to death." The Triangle fire unleashed a storm of protest among Americans interested in labor issues. As a result, existing protective laws were enforced and new safety standards enacted.

A year after the fire, in 1912, Rose Schneiderman spoke out in favor of women's right to vote. She was one of the few labor union women who campaigned actively for women's suffrage and she became famous as an orator. Schneiderman even argued before President Wilson, insisting: "The vote, Mr. President, is a necessity." In answer to the charge that women would "lose their beauty and purity if they voted," Rose said:

We have women working in the foundries stripped to the waist. . . . [Other women] stand for thirteen or fourteen hours in the terrible steam and heat with their hands in hot starch. Surely these women won't lose any more of their beauty and charm by putting a ballot in a ballot box once a year than they are likely to lose standing in foundries or laundries all year round.

Schneiderman never married. She devoted herself to improving the lives of working women and became one of the most prominent women in the labor movement. By 1918 she was president of the Women's Trade Union League. During the following years, she was chosen as a delegate to the First National Working Women's Congress in Washington, the Peace Conference in Paris, and the International Congress in Vienna.

In 1920, the year that women finally won the right to vote in the United States, Rose was chosen by the Farm Labor Party as their candidate for U.S. Senate. Although she did not win, she became one of the first women to run for such a high office.

Rose Schneiderman held her post at the Women's Trade Union League until her retirement in 1949. During that time she served as labor advisor to several government agencies. She was the only woman that President Franklin D. Roosevelt appointed to the Labor Advisory Board.

In her autobiography, *All for One*, Rose Schneiderman recounted her years of struggle in the labor movement. She died in 1961, but she is still remembered as a beacon of the trade union movement in the United States.

Rebekah Bettelheim Kohut

Rebekah Bettelheim came from a very different world than Rose Schneiderman, Clara Lemlich, and other poor Jewish factory workers. Yet she shared many of the same goals.

One of six children, Rebekah was born in Hungary in 1864 and came to the United States with her family when she was only two years old. Although her mother died quite young, Rebekah had heard many stories about how she had defied her community in Hungary by insisting on furthering her education. Rebekah's mother shocked them even more by becoming the first Jewish woman to teach school in Hungary. Rebekah later wrote: "Her example inspired me, led me as a young girl to seek out all kinds of less sheltered activities. . . ."

Rebekah's father also served as an inspiration for her. Albert Bettelheim was a physician and a rabbi. He served many congregations, and the family moved from one city to another. While in San Francisco, Rebekah attended the University of California.

Through her father she met her future husband, Alexander Kohut. A respected Hungarian rabbi, Kohut came to the United States in 1885 at the age of forty-three. Shortly afterwards, his first wife died, and he was left with eight children.

It was just at this time that Rebekah met Alexander Kohut. She admitted that she fell in love with him instantly. Never questioning any possible difficulties she might have raising another woman's children, Rebekah married Alexander in 1887. She quickly settled down in New York City as his wife and "other mother" to his children. The oldest stepchild was less than twelve years younger than Rebekah.

In her autobiography, *More Yesterdays*, Rebekah commented:

> *I was born for work and was unhappy unless I was getting more than my apportioned share of it. It must have been a contributing factor in my eagerness to marry Alexander Kohut. Having been given eight children at once, I didn't have to look for work; I had it.*

Rebekah Kohut never worked outside her home. The volunteer work she did was tentative and not entirely approved by her husband. Alexander did not prevent her from working as author and editor of the Jewish woman's journal, *Helpful Hints*. However, he pleaded with her not to attend the first Jewish Women's Congress in Chicago in 1893. Rebekah complied with his wishes and someone else read the paper she had prepared for the occasion. It was a discussion of how women's duties in the home and in the community were connected.

Rebekah was happy with Rabbi Kohut for seven years. When he died she was left a widow with the additional burden of supporting his children.

Faced with this new challenge, Rebekah never wavered. First, she gave a series of lectures on Jewish topics. Then she organized a girls' school and a summer camp. Although her school was not financially successful, her reputation as an educator gained her a job as director of the Columbia Grammar School.

These early activities launched Rebekah Kohut's professional career in the fields of education and social services. By 1914, she headed the Young Women's Hebrew Association Employment Service. She became known as an expert in the problems of the unemployed and from 1917 served on federal and state employment boards.

At the same time, Rebekah embarked on a career in the first Jewish women's club in America. The National Council of Jewish Women was modeled on Christian women's clubs. It was formed following the Jewish Women's Congress in Chicago in 1893. Hannah G. Solomon was the first president of the National Council of Jewish Women. The group expanded rapidly, forming local groups or chapters in many major cities. By 1897 Rebekah was president of the New York Chapter.

The National Council of Jewish Women had four aims: to study Judaism, to provide Sabbath Schools for the poor, to contribute money to the needy, and to act as a forum for the exchange of ideas among all Jewish women.

In New York City, under Rebekah's leadership, the commitment to help the needy was quickly put into practice. The council sent their members to meet the Jewish immigrants coming into New York harbor. Council women helped the newcomers find housing, work, or missing relatives. They provided homes for young women who came alone, so they would not be lured into prostitution. They worked with poor children of all religions, providing recreation rooms, vocational training, cultural activities, playgrounds, and milk stations. In the days before pasteurization, milk stations staffed by women volunteers were often the only places where pure, safe milk was available to city children.

"At the time the Council was founded," Rebekah recalled, "participation by women in public life was still a new thing, and there was an excitement, a heady sense of independence, a thrill, a feeling that one was taking part in the best kind of revolution."

Before Rebekah Kohut died at the age of eighty-seven, she had seen the eight Kohut children grow to be successful adults and had gained recognition as one of the great humanitarians of her time. At a banquet commemorating the fiftieth anniversary of the National Council of Jewish Women, nine hundred distinguished guests honored Rebekah Kohut. She was presented with a check of $50,000 to apply to any charities she chose.

Rebekah once called herself "a matriarch who never had any children of her own." However, she was loved and admired not only by the Kohut children and grandchildren, but by all who knew of her extraordinary commitment to the welfare of humanity.

Lillian Wald

Lillian Wald also devoted her life to helping poor people. Born in Cincinnati in 1867, she left a comfortable upper middle class home to live in the slums of New York City, where she provided nursing care and social services for immigrant workers.

Lillian was the third of four Wald children. Their father was a successful physician. However, Lillian was never expected to work. Raised in a wealthy area of Rochester, New York, where her family had moved, she was educated for marriage. Young women of her class were expected to entertain, call on friends, and go to charity balls.

This was not the life that Lillian wanted. Her dream was to assist her brother Albert. He would become a doctor and she would be his nurse, but those hopes were dashed when Albert was accidentally drowned.

Lillian searched for something to give meaning to her life. When she met a young nurse who had been called in to treat a family member, a new path was opened. She, too, could bring comfort and order into the homes of the sick and the poor.

It was not easy for Lillian's parents to accept her plan to leave home and go to Bellevue Nursing School. When they finally agreed, Lillian moved to New York City. She was twenty-two years old.

After graduating in 1891, Lillian chose to remain in New York City so she could help those most in need of her services. She began working in a hospital and taught courses in hygiene in the community. Then one day, a little girl approached her, took her by the hand, and led her into a world of poverty that she could never have imagined.

The child had called Nurse Wald to help her mother. In order to reach their home, Lillian had to walk through filthy, littered streets, and up a flight of slippery, mud-covered steps. Lillian never knew people could live in such squalid conditions.

"That morning's experience was a baptism of fire," she wrote. Lillian believed that if only the world knew how these people were living, conditions would change.

This incident inspired Lillian Wald and her colleague, Mary Brewster, to become the first public health nurses. They founded the Visiting Nurse Service. Through this service, nurses cared for the sick in their own homes, charging ten cents a visit or less, so that patients could keep their dignity. The service was not affiliated with any religion or charity.

The nurses lived among the people they served and worked wherever they were needed. They climbed up and down narrow, dark staircases and walked through alleyways filled with garbage. The patients they tended sometimes had only a plank for a bed.

Through the Visiting Nurse Service Lillian Wald learned more about the needs of her patients. In response, she gradually expanded her work. She created the Settlement House on Henry Street in a building purchased by the wealthy philanthropist, Jacob Schiff. There, she developed all kinds of services for the poor.

The Henry Street Settlement was the center of the Visiting Nurse Service. Other young, enthusiastic nurses joined the staff. Settlement House workers offered courses in health and child care, organized clubs for children, and taught English to immigrants.

Lillian Wald campaigned to create new laws to end the exploitation of workers. She was active in promoting the establishment of a Federal Children's Bureau in 1912. She fought for child labor legislation, a struggle that continued for many years. Not until 1938 did federal

Lillian Wald

law finally make it illegal to employ children under the age of fourteen.

After the Triangle Shirt Waist fire in 1911, Lillian Wald supported the Women's Trade Union League. She campaigned for state legislation to improve conditions in the sweatshops. Her commitment to unions created a rift between her and her principal benefactor, Jacob Schiff. Schiff complained that Nurse Wald should focus on her social work. Rather than risk the loss of funding from Schiff, Wald felt compelled to resign from the Women's Trade Union League.

Lillian Wald was a loving and caring woman whose warmth embraced almost everyone who met her. She had a loyal following of devoted professionals. They lived in the Settlement House and carried out the programs created there.

A group of wealthy people supported Wald's many causes with generous contributions. As the young people who benefited from her programs grew up and became successful, they also joined the ranks of contributors.

In 1913, on the twentieth anniversary of the Settlement House, ten thousand supporters thronged the neighborhood for the celebration. Important officials and judges attended. The Settlement was now a complex of seven buildings with a staff of ninety-two nurses. Lillian Wald's career was at its pinnacle.

With the outbreak of World War I in 1914, Lillian Wald joined other social reformers and labor leaders to campaign against the war. At first, the leaders of the peace movement were considered patriots, but as enthusiasm for the war increased, those who did not support it were condemned and denounced.

Lillian Wald was among the few who maintained that war was immoral and not worth the price of human life. As a result of this strong belief, she lost a great deal of financial support. Jacob Schiff was one of the few who continued giving her money, even when he disagreed with her political position.

With the end of the war, Wald regained some of her former influence. Once again she embarked on major fund raising campaigns. She wanted to ensure that the Henry Street Settlement and the Visiting Nurse Service would continue after her death. Although Lillian was never identified with any Jewish organization or religious group, her efforts were funded and supported by many Jews.

At her death in 1940, thousands mourned Lillian Wald. She was remembered at a service led by Rabbi Stephen S. Wise of the Free Synagogue. Thirty years later, Wald was inducted into the Hall of Fame for Great Americans. Her true legacy, however, lives on in the institutions and services that were inspired by her vision.

Emma Goldman

Emma Goldman was a Russian Jew, born in 1869 in the city of Kovno. Her parents struggled to make a living and had little time for their children. The emotional warmth offered by her half-sister Helena was the only love Emma felt throughout her harsh childhood.

When the family moved to St. Petersburg in 1882, Emma was exposed to revolutionary ideas. Talk of equality and freedom was everywhere. Books were secretly passed from one student to another. Emma, still in her early teens, became increasingly sympathetic to these ideals.

When she was fifteen, her father's grocery store could no longer provide enough support for the family. Emma had to take a job in a factory. Her parents were also pressing her to marry, but Emma resisted. Instead, she begged to be allowed to go to America with Helena.

By the end of 1885, Emma had crossed the ocean and was living in Rochester, New York. Here she quickly found work in another factory. The hours were long and the conditions oppressive — sometimes even worse than in Russia. Nevertheless, her parents and brothers joined her and her sisters in America.

An early marriage to Jacob Kirschner, a young immigrant, gave Emma the opportunity to leave her family. However, she quickly discovered that she had merely exchanged the oppression of her father for the oppression of her husband. Jacob refused to allow his young wife to work.

During this unhappy period, Emma read about the Haymarket Affair in the newspapers. The Haymarket Affair began at a workers' rally in May, 1886 at Haymarket Square in Chicago. During the rally a bomb exploded amid a group of policemen, killing seven and injuring many more. Eight prominent anarchists were arrested. The men were tried, found guilty, and a year later four of them were hanged.

Anarchists oppose any form of government or law. They are against the state because it imposes order by force. Emma Goldman felt drawn to the anarchists and their cause. She vowed to dedicate herself "to the memory of my martyred comrades."

Her new commitment pushed her to end her disastrous marriage and in 1889 she obtained a divorce. Soon afterwards, Emma Goldman picked up her sewing machine and headed for New York City.

In New York Emma contacted a political friend who brought her into a group of anarchists. She felt at home among these people and quickly became involved in radical circles. Tutored by famous anarchist speakers, Goldman was soon giving lectures all over the country. Many of her speeches were in Yiddish.

In 1892, Emma's friend and lover, Alexander (Sasha) Berkman, conceived of a plan to assassinate the wealthy businessman Henry Clay Frick. Sasha saw his act as a protest against Frick's oppression of steel workers in Pittsburgh. Although she later said she opposed violence, Emma raised money for Sasha.

The assassination attempt failed and Berkman went to prison for twenty-two years. Goldman remained loyal to him, sending books and food to his prison cell. However, she continued to pursue an active life, supporting herself by writing and lecturing.

Goldman became known as "Red Emma," the most famous and effective anarchist in the country. In 1893, when she urged unemployed, poverty-stricken workers to overthrow the political and economic system, she was jailed. Sent to a prison in New York City, she came in contact with prison doctors who encouraged her to become a practical nurse. When Emma was released ten months later, she resolved to get a nursing degree. This would give her a more secure way of earning a living. With financial help from an old friend, Emma traveled to Vienna where she obtained her degree and gained experience as a midwife.

Emma Goldman

was deported to

Russia because of

her political views.

Back in the United States, Goldman worked as a nurse and expanded her political activities. She lived with several different lovers, all anarchists. In 1906 she began publishing a radical journal called *Mother Earth*. Its aim was to show the injustices of American society.

"The Tragedy of Women's Emancipation" was one of Emma's most famous articles. She wrote that women had exchanged "the narrowness and lack of freedom of the home . . . for the narrowness and lack of freedom of the factory . . . or office." Emma did not support the women's suffrage movement, but she firmly believed that women should be able to control the number of children they had.

In the 1900s it was against the law to distribute any information on birth control. Although Emma had included this subject in previous lectures, she did not deal with specific methods. Now she supported Margaret Sanger, the only person providing women with birth control material.

This decision would eventually lead to Goldman's imprisonment. Emma was condemned for her views on anarchy, for refusing to marry the men with whom she lived, and for demonstrating how to use contraceptives.

Then came her opposition to World War I. In 1917 the Selective Service Act was passed. The purpose of this act was to draft young men for war. Emma denounced both the war and the draft. Together with Alexander Berkman, now out of prison, she made speeches and wrote anti-war articles in *Mother Earth*.

Emma was arrested, charged, and convicted of conspiracy to overthrow the Selective Service Act. She and Berkman were sent to prison where Emma expected to spend the rest of her life. She was forty-six years old.

Emma's prediction did not come true. Instead, she was deported to Russia under the Alien Exclusion Act of 1918. This law provided that any foreigner who advocated the overthrow of the government could be sent back to her or his country of origin.

Bitterly disappointed with Communism after a tour through the new Soviet Union, Emma spent her last years trying to return to the United States. She managed to obtain British citizenship in 1925 and eventually moved to Canada. In 1931 she wrote her autobiography, *Living My Life*.

By 1932 Emma recognized the threat of Nazism in Germany and made speeches throughout Europe and North America denouncing Hitler. Until her death in 1940, Emma Goldman never wavered from her basic belief in the inherent goodness of the working man. Asked to concentrate more on Jewish causes, she replied: "social injustice is not confined to my own race."

Till the end, Emma Goldman insisted that individual freedom was the most important thing in human society and that all government was a threat to that freedom.

Vitke Kempner Kovner (right) shown with other women partisans.

Heroines of the Holocaust

Worrld War I was the first armed conflict that involved most of Europe and North America. Nine million soldiers and more than 30 million civilians were killed in this war waged to "make the world safe for democracy." Yet, in spite of that promise, only twenty years later the world was once again at war.

There were many reasons why a second world war occurred. After losing World War I, Germany had been forced to sign the Versailles Treaty. This peace agreement deprived the German nation of large chunks of territory. Germany was also required to surrender most of its merchant ships and dismantle its army. These humiliations, added to the country's severe economic problems, prepared the groundwork for Adolf Hitler's policies.

Hitler and his supporters wanted to transform Germany into a great power once again. Another of Hitler's goals was to annihilate all the Jews of Europe.

First at home, and then in every other country Germany conquered, Nazi police and special army units separated the Jews from the gentile population. Jews were crowded into walled ghettos and forced to work for the Nazi war effort. Many starved to death or died of disease.

Beginning in 1942, those Jews who remained alive were sent to concentration camps in Eastern Europe where most were killed. Evidence shows that women perished at an even higher rate than men in these camps. They were particularly vulnerable as mothers; they might try to hide their pregnancies, or resist when their captors forcibly separated them from their young children. Women frequently suffered sexual assaults at the hands of Nazi persecutors. When World War II finally came to an end in 1945, six million Jews, a full one-third of the Jewish population of the world, had been destroyed.

As with every war, World War II had its heroes and heroines. Jews fought the Nazis at every turn and with different methods. In one of many acts of passive resistance, an entire *Beis Yaakov* school of young women decided to commit suicide. Had they lived, they would have been forced to become prostitutes for German soldiers.

Other Jews resisted by fighting to stay alive. Some fled to the forests and became partisans, guerrilla fighters against the Nazis. Small numbers hid with the help of friendly and courageous gentile families. Perhaps the most famous of these hidden families is known to us through the diary of Anne Frank, a twelve year old Jewish girl who loved to write. Anne recorded her feelings as a young woman growing up in hiding. She described the daily life of her family and the other people who were concealed with them in an attic in Amsterdam. They survived for over two years until they were discovered by the Nazis. Anne died of typhus in a concentration camp shortly before the Germans were defeated. Although her dream of becoming a famous writer was never fulfilled, she gained immortality through her diary.

The majority of European Jews, forced into ghettos, found other means of resistance. Children of nine or ten regularly slipped beyond the walls to smuggle in food for their starving families. In the face of death, cultural activities and schools were set up. Zionist groups organized, teaching the young to defend themselves with stolen weapons and homemade bombs. A few Jews secretly left the ghetto for short periods of time. They worked to sabotage Nazi plans and slow down efforts to deport Jews.

Women were often more valuable than men in these plots. Men had the visible mark of circumcision on their bodies. Without any sign of their Jewishness, it was easier for women to pass as Christians. By pretending to be friendly with German soldiers, young women might discover important information that would help to save Jews.

Countless Jewish women risked — or gave — their lives to fight the Nazis. Much of that heroism remains unrecorded. However, a few women stand out for their leadership and bravery in the face of tremendous odds.

Zivia Lubetkin Zuckerman

The bombing of Warsaw, Poland by the Germans marked the official beginning of World War II. Once the city was in German hands, the Jews were immediately in danger. As they would do in city after city throughout the war, the Nazis rounded up Warsaw's Jews and crowded them into one small area. From the beginning, groups of Jews, mostly in their teens and twenties, began to organize and resist the Germans. One of these young people was Zivia Lubetkin. Zivia was born in Beten, Poland, in 1914. From a young age, she was active in the Labor Zionist movement. She worked her way up in the organization to become a member of the executive council.

The year the war broke out, Zivia, then twenty-five years old, was attending the Zionist Congress in Geneva, Switzerland. Although she could have fled to the safety of Palestine, Zivia was determined to join her comrades in German-occupied Warsaw and share in the underground operations. Immediately after her return in 1940, she became active in planning an armed resistance against the Nazis.

Her activities earned Zivia the nickname "Mother of the Ghetto." She became so well known among the Jewish network of fighters that her name, Zivia, was used as a code word for Poland in secret messages. Inside the ghetto, she helped organize schools for children, lectures for adults, and new Zionist youth groups.

The motto of the ghetto fighters was: "To live with honor and to die with honor." Zivia and her comrades had no doubt that the Germans would kill the Jews. As long as they were alive, though, they insisted on living with dignity.

Zivia was regularly sent out of the Warsaw ghetto to warn other Jews of the fate in store for them. She urged them not to show up when the deportation orders came, to hide their children, and to resist the Germans.

During those trips outside the ghetto, she and other young women sometimes disguised themselves as Poles and pretended to flirt with the German soldiers. In this way, they hoped to gain information about troop movements or the arrival of shipments. They could sometimes steal a pistol or a stick of dynamite to bring back into the ghetto.

Finally, in April 1943, after several skirmishes with German soldiers, the ghetto fighters felt they had enough arms and ammunition. When they

Zivia Lubetkin was called "Mother of the Ghetto."

heard that the ghetto was to be liquidated, they began a major resistance against the Nazis.

The Nazi forces numbered 2,842 soldiers plus 7,000 extra police and secret service men. They had tanks, machine guns, and ammunition. The ghetto underground had only a few hundred young men and women, a small stash of stolen guns, and homemade bombs.

In spite of this, the determined Jewish fighters managed to drive the Germans out of the ghetto time after time. Other Jews joined them in a desperate effort to "die with honor."

Zivia later described her feelings during that historic battle, the very first citizen rebellion against the German army. "We had been amazed by our first victory over the enemy. We had been intoxicated and a feeling of pride had filled our hearts with his flight; he would not vanquish us so easily."

The Germans then tried a new tactic. Rather than face a house-to-house struggle, they set fire to the ghetto to force the fighters out. Although they knew they were doomed, Zivia and the others continued planning and fighting. Retreating from each building as the fire consumed it, the ghetto fighters, their numbers dwindling, held on. They hid in a bunker at number 18 Mila Street.

On May 8, the Germans discovered this last bunker and blew up all the entrances. Most of the remaining Jewish fighters, including the commander Mordecai Anielewicz, were killed. Zivia was not in the bunker during the attack. When she and a few others returned to 18 Mila and discovered what had happened, they made a heart-wrenching decision. It was time to escape.

Following a pre-arranged plan, the fifty remaining fighters climbed down into the Warsaw sewers. They carried their wounded comrades on their backs and tied their weapons around their necks. Zivia was chosen to lead the group.

Zivia Lubetkin later described the horror and exhaustion she experienced as they trudged for hours in the darkness, filth, and slime of the sewers. "My feet seemed to move automatically in this dark shaft, and the echoes of a remote dream returned . . . of the distant land of Israel . . . of a life of dignity."

Of those fifty survivors, only thirty-four escaped. Isaac (Antek) Zuckerman, one of the underground commanders already outside the ghetto, organized the rescue. A truck met the weary refugees as they emerged from the sewers into the street on the "Aryan side." They were whisked away to the safety of the forests.

When Warsaw Poles finally revolted against their German captors in 1944, these Jews came to join the battle. Until the end of the war, Zivia led guerrilla detachments in Poland. In 1946, she and Antek Zuckerman married and moved to Israel where they helped found Kibbutz *Lochamei HaGettaot*, the Kibbutz of the Ghetto Fighters.

Zivia thought that no one in Palestine knew of her bravery against the Nazis. However, reports of the Warsaw ghetto uprising spread quickly. In the newly independent Jewish state, Zivia was honored for her role in the defense of the Jewish people.

In 1978, she died, as she had lived, with honor.

Vitke Kempner Kovner

When Vitke Kempner was born, in 1920, no one expected her life to be filled with violence. In Kalish, the town near the Polish-German border where she lived, she received a traditional education. She studied Hebrew, the Bible, and Jewish history, as well as secular subjects. She became a Zionist and joined *HaShomer HaTzair*, the socialist Zionist youth movement.

After high school, Vitke continued her secular studies at Warsaw University. She was home for vacation in September, 1939 when Germany attacked Poland.

The first time the Germans assembled the Jews of Kalish for deportation, Vitke discovered she couldn't stand being a prisoner. Together with three young men, she jumped out of a window and escaped. The small group headed for Vilna, which was still a free city. There, Jews were able to get certificates to enter Palestine.

In Vilna, a major center of Jewish life, Vitke met Abba Kovner, the head of the central committee of the combined Zionist groups. Although Abba was only twenty-two, he was the one who decided which of the young people would go on to Palestine. Some had to stay behind to protect those not old enough to leave. Vitke was chosen to remain.

Vitke Kempner Kovner (left) led groups of Polish Jews to the safety of the forest.

Less than a year later, the Soviet Union took over Vilna. When the Russians began arresting all Jewish Zionists and sending them to Siberia, Vitke escaped again. She fled to a small Russian town and remained there until Germany invaded Russia in 1941.

Despite the dangers of travel during wartime, especially for Jews, Vitke decided to return to her comrades in Vilna. When she arrived, she could hardly believe what had happened. Thousands of Jews had been taken out of the city and murdered by the Nazis. The rest were forced into a walled ghetto.

Vitke had the opportunity to escape the ghetto and live in a convent where the nuns were sympathetic to Jews. However, if the destiny of the Jewish people was to die, she decided, "we have no right to save ourselves. If all the people are in the ghetto, we have to be in the ghetto and prepare for action."

The young people of *HaShomer HaTzair* and other youth groups prepared themselves to fight against the Germans. "Let us not be led like sheep to the slaughter," Abba Kovner proclaimed in a pamphlet. Vitke Kempner belonged to a small group of young Jews who organized into units and planned acts of sabotage against the Nazis.

Vitke carried the first bomb outside the ghetto walls and planted it on the railroad tracks. Time after time she slipped out with the work crews and returned in the same way. She spent many nights alone in the forests around Vilna, planning where to place bombs and figuring out how to escape.

Finally, in September of 1943, the Germans began deporting all the remaining Jews from the Vilna ghetto. Jews were either killed immediately or sent to concentration camps.

The tiny Jewish fighting force attempted armed resistance but failed. They decided to withdraw through the underground sewer pipes into the forest. One group was caught and killed but Vitke's group made it safely to Rudniki Forest. There they organized a partisan unit under the direction of Abba Kovner.

Women had played an important role as ghetto fighters. "It is easier for a woman to go in the streets and to be (unrecognized as a Jew)," explained Vitke in an interview long after the war. "Also the Germans did not suspect the women . . . All this *(sic)* really dangerous things, the women did."

Although some men complained about fighting alongside women, Abba Kovner insisted that women should be an active part of the resistance. Vitke continued her work sabotaging German trains and blowing up important targets. In addition to planting bombs, she rescued groups of Jews who remained hidden in the ghetto and led them to the safety of the forest.

When the war was over, Vitke was one of the handful of Jews from Vilna who still remained alive. It is estimated that approximately 100,000 Jews from the Vilna area died during the war.

Vitke and Abba Kovner married and settled in Israel where Abba Kovner became a writer and poet. Widowed in 1990, Vitke Kempner Kovner continues to live a quiet life in Kibbutz *Ein HaHoresh*. Recalling her days as a partisan, Vitke said: "It is what I think is my most important job, to bring Jewish people to the forest. I think, if I am proud about something . . . I am proud that I did this."

Gisella Perl

Gisella Perl was born in Transylvania, a province of Rumania, in 1910. She grew up during the brief years of peace between the two world wars and studied to become a doctor — a rarity for a woman in those years. When Germany invaded Poland in 1939, she was married, had a son and daughter, and was working as an obstetrician/gynecologist.

Although Rumania is not very far from Poland, Gisella's life did not change much for a full year after the invasion. Then, in 1940, northern Transylvania was annexed by Hungary, an ally of Nazi Germany. Almost immediately, the Nazis began herding Transylvanian Jews into ghettos. Despite the lack of food and medical supplies, Gisella continued practicing medicine.

Then the transports began. Each day, groups of Jews were rounded up, placed in boxcars with no food or water, and taken to Auschwitz, a concentration camp in Poland. Although they were told they were being relocated in order to work, most suspected they were going to be killed.

In March, 1944 Gisella, her husband, and her parents were transported to Auschwitz. Her mother and father were immediately killed. The younger men and women were separated. Gisella would never see her husband again.

In a book written after the war, Gisella described how most of those who arrived on the transports were gassed to death and then burned in large crematoria. Those who were not killed immediately often died of starvation, disease, or from beatings at the hands of Nazi guards.

Even though Auschwitz was a death camp, there was a hospital in it, and Gisella Perl, now prisoner 25404, became one of the doctors. Without instruments, drugs, or even clean bandages, she treated patients, sometimes even performed operations, "on a dirty floor, using only my dirty hands." Gisella always tried to encourage other prisoners with promises for a better future. The prisoners loved her and called her "Gisi doctor."

One of Gisella's main jobs in the camp was to perform abortions on pregnant women. "No one will ever know what it meant to me to destroy those babies," she told a reporter much later. "But if I had not done it, both mother and child would have been cruelly murdered."

No doctor's efforts could prevent thousands from dying, however. When Gisella first arrived in Auschwitz, she lived with 32,000 other Polish and Hungarian women. Six months later, by September, 1944, only 10,000 of these women remained alive.

Almost an entire year passed in the nightmare called Auschwitz. By January, 1945 rumors that the Germans were losing the war began to spread. Gisella was transferred by train to a prison hospital for slave laborers in Hamburg, Germany. Although conditions were terrible, "it was heaven compared to Auschwitz." Gisella treated prisoners wounded in the allied bombing raids.

With the war almost over, Gisella, along with other prisoners, was evacuated by truck from the burning city of Hamburg. She was taken to another camp: Bergen Belsen. There, among heaps of corpses, she found the bodies of her brother and sister.

Surrounded by death and dying, Gisella Perl worked in the Maternity Block. On April 15, 1945, as the British troops were marching into the camp, she delivered "the first free child born in Bergen Belsen."

Dr. Perl remained in Bergen Belsen for a while, treating the recovering prisoners and delivering their babies. Then she left to try and find the remains of her family. Tragically, she discovered that her husband and son had both been killed just before the war ended.

Discouraged and overwhelmed by her years of suffering, Gisella tried to commit suicide, but she was found in time for her life to be saved. In a convent outside Paris, she finally regained her health.

It took many more years for the spiritual wounds to heal. Calling herself the "ambassador for the six million," Gisella Perl traveled throughout America speaking to doctors and other professional groups about her experiences. One day she met Eleanor Roosevelt, widow of President Franklin D. Roosevelt. Mrs. Roosevelt advised Gisella: "Stop torturing yourself. Become a doctor again."

With the help of American friends, Dr. Perl was granted U.S. citizenship and set up a practice in New York City. She became an expert in helping women to become pregnant.

In 1979, just before her seventieth birthday, Gisella Perl moved to Israel. There, she was reunited with her daughter Gabrielle, who, hidden by a Christian family, had survived the war. In 1982, Dr. Perl was honored by the National Women's Division of *Shaare Zedek* hospital in Jerusalem where she donated her time to the gynecological clinic.

Gisella Perl is one of many heroines who survived the horrors of war. Through strength of character and commitment, she was able to overcome tragedy and make a lasting contribution to her people and the world.

Hannah Szenes

Aniko Szenes (Senesh) was born in Budapest, Hungary, in 1921, into a prosperous, assimilated family. Her father, a well-known playwright, died young and Aniko's mother, Kato, raised her and her brother alone.

Hungary had once been part of the Austro-Hungarian Empire. This great empire had granted Jews equality in the early part of the nineteenth century. One hundred years later, the political situation was very different. After siding with Germany in World War I, Hungary, though still independent, was small and impoverished.

By the 1930s, Hungary was following Germany's lead and becoming a fascist state. Fascism was the form of government already adopted by Germany and Italy. Under fascism a dictator has total political power and forcibly suppresses all opposition.

Once it became fascist, Hungary, too, began passing anti-Semitic laws. Jews were barred from universities and were not allowed to be officers in private clubs. As the fascists gained more power, anti-Semitic restrictions became more vicious and oppressive. In this atmosphere, opportunities for young Jews were clearly limited.

While still in her teens, Aniko found her way into the Zionist movement. She learned Hebrew and prepared for a life working the soil. When she sailed for Haifa, Germany had already annexed Austria and had just invaded Poland, but the war still seemed far from Hungary.

In *Eretz Israel*, Aniko changed her name to Hannah, the Hebrew equivalent. She began by studying agriculture at the Nahalal farm school for girls. The principal of that school was Hannah Meisel, the pioneer who had set up the very first training school for girls twenty-seven years before. When Hannah Szenes was not working or studying, she wrote letters home, kept a diary, and composed poetry and plays.

After graduating from the Nahalal training school, Hannah joined a group of young people who were preparing to start a new kibbutz. She worked hard, but as the war spread throughout Europe, Hannah worried about her family.

Hannah knew her brother Gyuri was trapped in France when it was taken over by the Nazis. She worked hard to obtain official papers for Gyuri and her mother so they could join her in Palestine, but it was becoming more difficult to leave Europe every day.

Despairing over the fate of her loved ones, Hannah learned that the British were training a group of Jews to return to Europe. Their job would be to aid in the planned attack by British and American troops and to help save the remaining Jews of Hungary. Along with several male friends, Hannah volunteered.

Hannah spoke Hungarian and knew the country well, but had no military experience. She waited anxiously to find out if she would be accepted. After months of waiting, the answer came. Yes. She could join a small group of men who were being sent to Cairo for training. From there, the group would parachute into Yugoslavia where partisans would help them cross the border.

The hardest part of the mission was waiting in Yugoslavia for the go-ahead. The Nazis had finally overtaken Hungary in 1944 and were working feverishly to deport as many Jews as possible. Although it was clear that Germany was losing the war, they were more and more anxious to win their campaign against the Jews. In twenty-three days, 289,000 Hungarian Jews had been burned in Auschwitz. A month later, the number of murdered Hungarian Jews had risen to 437,402.

As this news reached the small group waiting across the border, Hannah became more desperate. She could wait no longer. She insisted on crossing into Hungary, alone if necessary, before it was too late. Finally, she convinced the others.

Before she left, she handed one of her comrades a piece of paper. "Here," she said, "just in case." Written out in Hebrew was a short poem, now the most famous of all Hannah's writing:

> *Blessed is the match consumed in kindling flame.*
>
> *Blessed is the flame that burns in the secret fastness of the heart.*
>
> *Blessed is the heart with strength to stop its beating for honor's sake.*
>
> *Blessed is the match consumed in kindling flame.*

During the night Hannah and three refugees who had just escaped from Hungary crossed the border. The others, the group from Palestine, would follow. They agreed to meet in Budapest in a week, but that meeting never took place.

Hannah and the three other men were quickly captured by the Germans and taken to prison in Budapest. Under torture, Hannah revealed her true identity and her mother was arrested and brought to prison.

The two women remained in a German prison for a long time. Then Hannah's mother, Kato, was released. The situation seemed to be improving. Hannah was no longer being tortured or kept in solitary as she had been when she was first caught. Friends and relatives were waiting for the Germans to be driven out of Hungary by the advancing Russian and English troops. It was only a matter of time.

Kato obtained a gentile lawyer for her daughter. He assured her that Hannah would get only a few years in prison and would be released as soon as allied forces took over.

In spite of these reassurances, one morning just before the Nazis withdrew from Budapest, they took Hannah Szenes out of the prison into the courtyard and shot her to death. Hannah was brave until the end. Refusing the traditional blindfold, she faced down her murderers and died defying them.

After her death most of Budapest was destroyed in a vicious battle between the German and Russian armies. Hannah's mother, Kato, managed to escape from the last forced transport and returned to her native city. When the war was over, she was contacted by Palestinian officials. After much waiting, she joined a group of refugees with legal permission to settle in Palestine. There, she was reunited with her son, Gyuri, who had managed to reach safety just before Hannah left for Europe.

Some years later, Hannah's body was transported to the new state of Israel. She received full honors and is buried in Jerusalem alongside many other great Jewish heroes.

Hannah Szenes,

in a desperate

attempt to save Jews,

parachuted into

Europe.

Bertha Kalich was a great star of the Yiddish theater.

Chapter 18

Extending the Boundaries

After World War II, the world began to change more rapidly. Technological advances made atomic energy and space travel a reality. Computers opened up undreamed-of possibilities. Methods of communication — from telegraph to television to transoceanic telephone lines — became more efficient.

Along with these scientific developments, ideas also changed. Women began to think differently about themselves. Many were no longer content to remain in the background: not in politics, nor in the work place, nor in family life. Some wanted full equality with men.

In the nineteenth century, women's desire for equality had inspired a major movement for women's suffrage. In the United States, after a long struggle, a constitutional amendment granted women the right to vote in 1920.

With that victory, more Jewish women became successful. They worked as social workers, organizers, and activists. By the early twentieth century, Jewish women were also forging careers in the arts and sciences and even in the predominantly male professions of law, medicine, and banking. In the performing arts, a significant number of Jewish women found new ways to express a commitment to Judaism.

Bertha Kalich, for example, was a dramatic actress born in 1875. She began her acting career on the Yiddish stage in Poland.

Later she became a Broadway success, but her Yiddish-speaking characters were always closest to her heart. Kalich died in 1939, just before World War II destroyed the Jewish communities of Eastern Europe and the Yiddish theater that she loved.

Sophie Tucker was an American Jewish cabaret and vaudeville singer in the years between the two world wars. She "belted out"songs like "My Yiddishe Mama" and "Some of These Days" to sell-out crowds. Highly successful, Tucker was always identified with her Jewish origins. Before she died in 1966, she established two youth centers in Israel, both named after her.

Jewish women gradually began to make their marks in law and finance, also. Fanny Holtzman, raised by immigrant parents, was the only woman in the Fordham Law School class of 1922. She became a nationally famous lawyer and advisor to Hollywood movie stars and celebrities. Before World War II, Holtzman worked hard to help rescue European Jews from the threat of Hitler and Nazism.

Shortly after the war, a young Jewish girl named Muriel Siebert came to New York City from her hometown of Cleveland, Ohio. Without a college degree or family connections, she found work as an assistant researcher for a stock brokerage firm. Thirteen years later Muriel became the first woman to hold a seat on the New York Stock Exchange. In 1977 the governor of New York appointed Siebert Superintendent of Banking. She guided the state through one of its worst banking crises.

Despite these pioneering efforts, however, opportunities for women were still far from being equal.

Rosalyn Sussman Yalow

A few women had made important contributions to science and medicine in the past. The most famous woman scientist, Madame Marie Curie, was a Polish-born French physicist. She won the Nobel Prize in 1903 for her discovery of radium and polonium. In 1911 she won a second Nobel Prize in chemistry. Marie Curie became a role model for Rosalyn Sussman.

Rosalyn was born in 1921, a year after women were first allowed to vote, and lived in the South Bronx, a modest section of New York City. Her father, Simon, owned his own small business selling cardboard and twine, but the family had few luxuries.

Although she was an outstanding math student, Rosalyn's teachers recognized her special aptitude in chemistry. They encouraged her to seek a career in that field, assuming she would work instead of getting married.

Before the Women's Rights Movement of the 1960s, it was rare for a woman to combine career and marriage. But Rosalyn had different ideas. By the time she graduated from Walton Girls High School, at fifteen, she had decided that she would marry and also be a scientist.

Rosalyn entered Hunter College, a free city university for women, as a chemistry major. At Hunter, Rosalyn took physics for the first time. Her teachers recognized that she excelled even more in physics than in chemistry. They advised her to concentrate on physics. After graduating in January, 1941 with top honors, Rosalyn searched for a graduate program that would accept her and give her financial aid.

Despite her excellent grades, one school after another rejected Rosalyn Sussman. A midwestern university candidly explained the reason for the rejection. As a Jew and a woman, she would never get a job!

Rosalyn decided to accept a secretarial job at Columbia University. As an employee of the school, she would be allowed to take courses for free.

Then, at the end of summer in 1941, a letter came that changed everything. Rosalyn was accepted at the University of Illinois at Urbana. Was it because so many men were being drafted that there was room for a woman? Or had she impressed someone on the admissions committee? Rosalyn would never be sure, nor did the reason matter. She had received a teaching assistantship and could support herself while studying.

At Urbana, Rosalyn Sussman was the only woman among four hundred faculty and teaching assistants, and one of only three Jews. One of the other Jews was a man named Aaron Yalow.

Aaron, the son of an Orthodox rabbi from New York, entered the physics program when Rosalyn did. They became friends and by 1943 were married.

After receiving their Ph.D.s, Rosalyn and Aaron Yalow returned to the Bronx and found work together at a federal laboratory. When the laboratory closed, Rosalyn taught physics at Hunter College, but her dream was to find work as a researcher.

Dr. Rosalyn S. Yalow was the first woman educated wholly in the United States to win the Nobel Prize.

When her husband began working in the field of medical physics at Montefiore Hospital, he suggested that Rosalyn look into research positions there. She eventually met Dr. Bernard Roswit of the Bronx Veterans Administration (V.A.) Hospital. Impressed with Yalow's abilities, personality, and determination, Roswit offered her laboratory space and a modest salary.

Rosalyn began experimenting with the safe use of radioisotopes in humans. Radioisotopes were considered an inexpensive substitute for radium and were being used to treat cancer patients. Rosalyn suspected they might have other uses as well, but she was an expert in physics and needed a partner who had medical experience. Rosalyn chose Dr. Solomon Berson, a bright young doctor. They began an association that would last for twenty-two years.

During those early years at the V.A. laboratory, Rosalyn gave birth to her first son, Benjamin. She was back at work a week later, nursing her baby and learning to get along on little sleep. When her daughter Elanna came along, she followed the same schedule.

Rosalyn worked hard not to neglect her children or her work. She came home for lunch every day and maintained a traditional kosher home — all the while working at her laboratory sixty to eighty hours a week.

The original research with radioisotopes that Yalow and Berson did led them to the discovery of radioimmunoassay (RIA). RIA is a radioactive method of measuring chemical or biological substances with radioisotopes. It is so sensitive that it can measure any trace material, no matter how small the amount. With this technique hundreds of different hormones, viruses, and chemicals could be measured.

In 1959 the partners presented their discovery. Gradually, the scientific community began to realize the importance of RIA and the many different ways it could be used. Yalow and Berson's new technique caused "an explosion of knowledge" in every aspect of medicine.

After Berson died of a heart attack in 1972, Rosalyn continued alone. She published sixty papers and won many medical awards, including the Albert Lasker Prize for Basic Medical Research, in 1976. Dr. Yalow was the first woman to receive that prestigious prize.

The following year, 1977, at 6:45 A.M. the telephone rang. The voice at the other end informed Dr. Rosalyn Yalow that she had won half of the Nobel Prize for her work in discovering and developing RIA. The other half was won by two different male scientists for their discoveries concerning the hypothalamic area of the brain.

Yalow was the second woman Nobel laureate to be awarded the prize for physiology or medicine and the first female winner to be educated wholly within the United States.

Dr. Yalow refused to allow her fame to change her. She continued to work at the Bronx V.A. Hospital for a modest salary. In her laboratory, Yalow trained young scientists from all over the world. Proud of her accomplishments, she never regretted not patenting RIA. Although a patent would have made her rich, Rosalyn explained that she feels uncomfortable having "more money than I can spend usefully."

The real key to happiness, says Yalow, is doing what you want. Dr. Yalow continues to do what she loves best: scientific research. Her contribution to medical physics has made her a respected and famous scientist.

Louise Berliawsky Nevelson

Louise Berliawsky was born in Kiev, Russia in 1899. When she was six years old, the family immigrated to the United States. They settled in Rockport, Maine where Louise's father established a lumber business.

Louise was different from the American children in this small New England town. She came from another country and her parents spoke little English. She often felt excluded. Despite this, Louise participated in many high school activities. Outside of school, Louise took dance lessons and studied piano, but her favorite activity was always art.

From the time she was seven, Louise knew she would be a sculptor. She used to collect scraps of wood from her father's woodworking shop to use for art projects. Wandering along the seashore, she picked up driftwood.

Louise never wanted to have a traditional life as a wife and mother. She married the Russian Jewish shipowner, Charles Nevelson, so she would be able to leave Rockport and begin her career as an artist. Charles was fifteen years older than Louise and a successful New York businessman.

At first, Charles agreed that Louise should have her creative freedom. However, when their son Michael was born in 1922, things changed. The family moved to a suburb, far from the art world. Louise felt useless and unhappy.

Louise Nevelson always created a dramatic appearance.

When Michael was two years old, Louise took painting classes and became involved in the art world again. She decided she needed to go to Europe to study.

Louise and Charles separated and Michael was sent to his grandmother in Rockport. He went to the local school and learned woodworking from his grandfather.

With her parents' encouragement and help, Louise traveled to Europe several times. She studied with many different artists and sculptors but gained no recognition for her work.

Not until 1941, when she was forty-two years old, did Louise have her first art show in New York City. Although nothing sold, the reviews were favorable. Karl Nierendorf, the gallery owner, recognized her talent and arranged for more shows. Again, there were good reviews, but no sales.

Those were difficult years for Louise. The United States was still at war and her son Michael was far away, serving in the Merchant Marines. While she was working on her third show, her mother died. Then right after the war, Louise's father passed away. A year later, Karl Nierendorf, the man who had first recognized her as a great artist, also died.

Through all these painful events, Louise Nevelson never stopped working. Still striving for the success she knew she deserved, she experimented with new styles and new materials. In addition to wood, she tried Plexiglas, aluminum and other metals. She was strongly influenced by several trips to Mexico, where she first encountered Mexican art and archeology.

In 1955, Louise began showing her work regularly in one-woman shows. At last Louise's sculptures began to sell and to appear in major museums.

Bolstered by her success, Nevelson worked around the clock. She created all kinds of complicated sculptures which she called "environments." They were made from odd bits of wood, packing crates, and pieces of furniture. Painted in black, white, or gold, these "environments" made a lasting impression in the art world.

One of Louise Nevelson's major environments was a piece called "Homage 6,000,000." She created this work, a giant wall, painted black, with huge wooden spools and other shapes. It was a memorial to the six million Jews who died during World War II. After it was completed, Louise donated this environment to the Israel Museum in Jerusalem.

With age and success, Louise Nevelson became even more of a non-conformist. She loved to wear striking outfits, antique clothing, and long false eyelashes.

It was not unusual for Louise, dressed in a long silk robe and a dramatic hat, to be seen rummaging in the trash. Several months later, her trash treasure would become part of a new sculpture.

Nevelson used her energies on behalf of a variety of causes and charities. When Russia refused to allow Jews to emigrate to the free world, she worked to help them escape Communist oppression.

Always dramatic and outgoing, Louise thrived on travel, parties, and love affairs. She was active as an artist into her eighties. In 1985, when she was eighty-six years old, she was awarded the National Medal for the Arts. Louise Nevelson continued working until her death three years later.

Betty Goldstein Friedan

By 1940, World War II had brought many more women into the work force. Yet, the goal of equality had still not been reached. Then in 1963, a book, written by a Jewish woman named Betty Friedan, moved the Western world toward a new social revolution.

Betty Goldstein was born in Peoria, Illinois in 1921, almost twenty years before World War II. Her father owned a jewelry store. He was successful enough to send Betty, her sister, Amy, and her brother, Harry, to college.

Betty graduated from Smith, a prestigious women's college, with honors in psychology. Instead of taking an advanced degree, though, she chose to move to New York City and became a reporter for a small union newspaper.

Because so many men were serving in the Army in the 1940s, finding a job was not very difficult. When the war ended in 1945, however, Betty was immediately laid off and replaced by a man. This happened to many women during those post-war years. Some were happy to go back home and assume the role of wife and mother. Others began to search for new jobs and outlets for their talents and energies.

Betty, not yet married, had to support herself. She soon found a different job with the same newspaper. When she did marry, in 1947, she needed to continue working. Her husband, Carl Friedan, could not support them both. After she had children, Betty still wanted the challenge of a job outside her home.

Although many sociologists and psychologists insisted that women were happiest with domestic work and child care, Betty was not. She did freelance writing and kept busy with volunteer programs in her children's school.

At her fifteenth college reunion in 1957, Betty was asked to prepare a

Betty Friedan is considered by many to be the "mother" of the women's movement.

questionnaire for her class. Were the graduates of Smith happy? Did they put their education to good use? She hoped to use the results of these questions to write an article for a woman's magazine. She wanted to disprove the accepted belief that women did not need college for their "natural" domestic work. Betty would show that a college education was good for women.

When her classmates answered the questions, Betty was shocked. She found that, like herself, many of them felt unfulfilled with their lives. "Is this all there is?" they were asking themselves.

Betty never wrote her article. Instead, she researched "the problem that has no name" for five years. The result was her first book, *The Feminine Mystique*, published in 1963. *The Feminine Mystique* explained that it was not enough for most women to be "Tommy's mother" or "John's wife." They also had to discover their own needs and fulfill themselves.

At first, *The Feminine Mystique* was very controversial. Some saw Betty Friedan as a threat to family life. As more women began to read the book, her ideas slowly gained popularity.

When Betty toured the United States, speaking about her ideas, she was often laughed at and heckled. The press made fun of her and called her "the feminine mistake." Betty Friedan stood her ground. She faced hundreds of hostile crowds and became a leader of a new movement. It was called feminism or women's liberation.

Friedan helped organize and was the first president of the National Organization for Women (NOW). NOW's purpose was to help women fight for equality. After stepping down as President, Betty directed the first March for Women's Equality in August 1970. Organized in several major cities, the March was an overwhelming success.

In New York City alone, more than 10,000 women joined the March for Equality. Secretaries and housewives, lawyers and typists, waitresses and writers, all linked arms to show their unity. They carried banners proclaiming "Equal Rights to Jobs and Education" and "Political Power to Women."

After 1970, federal legislation helped women gain more rights. In addition, women started support groups, set up child care for working mothers, and sued employers for equal pay. Women created their own magazines, ran for public office, and returned to school in large numbers.

Gradually, Betty was pushed aside by the women's movement she had helped to create. As feminism grew away from her, some accused her of not keeping up with changing ideas. Others blamed her abrasive personality.

During the 1970s and 1980s, Betty developed in new directions. Her three children were grown and Betty was divorced from her husband Carl. She lectured at universities and wrote several books.

Betty had always been keenly aware of her Judaism. As a young girl, being Jewish in a mostly

Christian town like Peoria meant she could not join the high school sororities or date the boys in her class. Her parents could not join Peoria's country club.

In New York City, she became more comfortable with her Jewish identity. She shared Passover seders and other holiday celebrations with friends.

As she grew older, Betty began to study her Jewish heritage. She visited Israel and attended conferences on Jewish women and Jewish law. In 1985, while teaching at the University of Southern California, Friedan joined a Jewish study group led by Rabbi Laura Geller.

By the late 1980s, Betty was rediscovered by a new generation of feminists who saw her as the "mother" of the women's movement. In 1988, twenty-five years after *The Feminine Mystique* was published, Friedan was once more invited to speak, appear on television, and provide articles for feminist publications. She also wrote another book, *The Fountain of Age*, about women, men, and aging. It was published in 1993, when Betty was seventy-two.

Betty still teaches at universities and lectures all over the country. She continues to be an active participant in conferences, symposia, and television debates on women's issues.

Ruth Bader Ginsburg

By the mid-1970s, with the idea of women's equality gaining credibility, the number of women practitioners in law increased. The career of Ruth Bader, however, began long before feminist ideas had become accepted in American society. She fought hard to succeed in the legal profession.

Ruth was born into a family of Jewish immigrants from central Europe and Russia. Her father Nathan was a furrier who earned just enough to support his family.

Ruth's mother Celia was a strong and intelligent woman. In 1933, however, the year that Ruth was born, it was not acceptable for a married woman to work. If she did, it was assumed that her husband could not earn enough to maintain his family. Instead, Celia channeled her energies into her daughter, Ruth.

From her mother, Ruth learned to love reading and languages. Although Celia died in 1950, on the day of Ruth's graduation from high school, she continued to be a force in her daughter's life.

As a student Ruth excelled in both public and Hebrew school. She was active in clubs and honor societies, was a cheerleader, and played cello in the orchestra at James Madison High School in Brooklyn.

Her high grades won Ruth a scholarship to Cornell University. She graduated in 1954 with a degree in government and membership in Phi Beta Kappa, the academic honor society. Ruth

Ruth Bader Ginsburg

overcame many

barriers to become

the second woman

justice of the

U.S. Supreme Court.

put off further study to marry her college sweetheart, Martin Ginsburg.

Martin had graduated from Cornell a year earlier and was enrolled at Harvard Law School. In 1954, he was drafted into the army. Immediately after their marriage, Ruth followed Martin to Fort Sill, Oklahoma. When he was discharged two years later, the couple returned to Boston with their baby daughter, Jane.

Having a one-year-old child did not stop Ruth from pursuing her goals. She was accepted at Harvard Law School, one of nine women in a class of over five hundred. Determined to excel, she earned the nickname "Ruthless Ruthie."

In his last year of law school Martin became ill with cancer. Ruth copied all his notes for him and typed his papers. She did this while continuing her own studies and working on the Harvard Law Review.

When Martin took a job with a New York law firm, Ruth transferred to Columbia University for her final year. She was at the top of her class both at Harvard and Columbia when she graduated in 1959.

However, honors and high grades were not enough when it came time to look for a job. Ginsburg applied for law clerkships only to be told by judges that they would not work with a woman.

Although she did finally get a clerkship with Edmund L. Palmieri, a federal district judge in New York, Ruth still could not get a job at a law firm. In 1961, law firms simply did not hire women.

Instead, Ruth Bader Ginsburg spent two years at Columbia Law School working on an international project. She helped rewrite and translate the Swedish

Judicial Procedure Code. She then taught at Rutgers University Law School, one of the few women to become a professor at an American law school.

While at Rutgers, Ruth gave birth to her son James during summer vacation. Because women were usually fired when they became pregnant, Ruth had to hide her condition.

Despite her initial inability to find a job, and her need to conceal her pregnancy, Ruth never saw herself as a victim of sex discrimination. Then she read *The Second Sex*, written by a French woman, Simone de Beauvoir. First published in 1949, *The Second Sex* examines the different ways in which women are oppressed solely because they are women.

Ruth began to view her own professional problems in a different light. She became an advocate for the equal status of women and men under the law. As Ruth was becoming more sensitive to these issues, other women were also beginning to complain of sex-based prejudice.

In 1972, Professor Ginsburg returned to Columbia Law School as the school's first tenured female professor. At about the same time, she helped create the Women's Rights Project of the American Civil Liberties Union (ACLU) and argued six cases before the U.S. Supreme Court. She won all but one of the cases. By basing her arguments on the U.S. Constitution's equal protection principle, she helped end sex-based classifications within the law.

One case Ginsburg argued for the ACLU concerned pregnant women in the work force. As a result of her appeal, a new law prevented teachers from being fired if they became pregnant.

In June 1980, President Jimmy Carter nominated Ginsburg to the U.S. Court of Appeals for the District of Columbia. During her thirteen years on the bench, she wrote three hundred opinions, covering some of the most important social issues facing the United States.

Ginsburg explained the law concerning abortion rights and made judgments on the rights of homosexual men and women. She wrote opinions on affirmative action, the policy designed to help minorities gain equal opportunities in work and education.

When President Bill Clinton sought to nominate a new Supreme Court Justice in 1993, Judge Ginsburg's brilliant record made her an outstanding choice. She received the highest rating from the American Bar Association and her nomination was approved by a vote of ninety-six to three. Ruth Bader Ginsburg thus became the second woman to be appointed to the Supreme Court, and the first Jew to serve on the High Court since 1969.

When asked how she felt being the second woman to become a Supreme Court Justice, Judge Ginsburg responded: "It felt great, but it will be even grander when we stop counting."

In her acceptance speech, the newest Supreme Court Justice thanked her family, friends, and colleagues. Her most memorable thank you, however, was for her mother, Celia, "the bravest and strongest person I have known."

Judith Resnick

Distinguished professionals like Ruth Bader Ginsburg and Rosalyn Yalow could not credit feminism for their accomplishments. With sheer determination they broke into almost exclusively male fields before the women's movement. Astronaut Judith Resnick's career, on the other hand, would not

Judith Resnick worked

hard to become one

of the first women

astronauts to go

into space.

have been possible without the work of the women's movement.

Judith Resnick was born in 1949 in Akron, a small city in Ohio. Judy's father, Marvin, was an optometrist. Her mother, Sarah, worked as a legal secretary until she married. Together with her grandparents, Judith and her parents celebrated Sabbaths and holidays.

Judith was expected to excel and she did, especially in math. In Hebrew school she was also a top student. By the time Judith graduated from high school in 1966, the National Organization for Women (NOW) had already been organized. Young girls were demanding entry into the top science high schools and the all-male universities.

Although not involved in this struggle, Judith benefited from it. With an A+ average and top SAT scores, she was accepted to Carnegie Mellon University, where she majored in electrical engineering. Judith went on to earn a master's degree and a Ph.D. at the University of Maryland.

After a brief marriage Judith Resnick was at a crossroads. Recently divorced and at the end of her graduate work, she was ready for a new challenge.

For the first time, as a result of pressure from the women's movement, the

National Aeronautics and Space Administration (NASA) was actively recruiting women for the space program. "I'm going to try to be an astronaut," Judith told her father.

One thousand women answered that call in 1977. What could Judith do to increase the odds of being chosen? First, she began an exercise regimen to improve her physical stamina. Next, she got a pilot's license. She read everything she could find about the astronauts and their training.

Judith passed the NASA physical and became one of two hundred women competing for entry into the program. In January 1978, when the final selections were made, Judith Resnick was one of four women chosen. Sally Ride was the first American woman to go into space. Judith Resnick became the second woman and the first Jew to travel in space.

After almost six years of specialized training and hard work, Judith's mission was scheduled. She would be part of the crew of the space shuttle Discovery.

Following months of delays, the flight was launched on August 30, 1984. Discovery orbited the earth ninety-six times and landed five days later, on September 5, 1984.

Resnick, now a veteran astronaut, looked forward to her next assignment. It came two years later. But this time, Judith would not be the only woman in the crew. Christa McAuliffe, a New Hampshire school teacher, was chosen to be the first non-astronaut to go into space.

The Challenger crew trained for almost a full year. Weather problems, technical breakdowns, and human errors postponed takeoff several times.

On January 28, 1986, at 11:38 A.M., Challenger finally lifted off. Seventy-three seconds later, the space shuttle exploded. The people watching from the ground were horrified to see the Challenger disappear in a cloud of smoke. Everyone on board was killed.

In Akron, Ohio, Judith Resnick's grieving relatives and friends assembled to pay tribute to the first Jewish astronaut. The governor of Ohio came, too, to honor Judith. He said: "She knew she would be at home in space. And she was. And she is."

Judith Resnick's commitment to excellence and achievement has made it easier for young women to say: "When I grow up I want to be an astronaut." Judith never wanted to be remembered as the "woman astronaut," or the "Jewish astronaut." She just wanted to be an astronaut.

Women academics and students buying books at the Jewish Women's Caucus, a subgroup of the Association for Jewish Studies.

Chapter 19

Opening the World of Scholarship

For centuries, women had been excluded from Jewish learning. Although a handful of women did manage to become educated in Jewish law and literature, they were exceptional. Most were either the daughters of rabbis or from very learned families. Even when they were educated, women were rarely exposed to an in-depth study of talmudic or other legal texts. Law and liturgy (the texts of prayers) remained the private world of Jewish men.

By the twentieth century, however, a growing number of Jewish women were becoming highly educated in Jewish fields. Although there are many whose names could be mentioned, a few women emerge as dynamic and exciting thinkers and writers. The bare facts of their lives only hint at their powerful personalities and commitments. They used their intellectual abilities to explore different aspects of Jewish life.

One of the most unique among them was Trude Weiss-Rosmarin. A rebel from her earliest years, Trude Weiss was born in Frankfurt, Germany in 1908. Though they were religious, her middle class parents did not see the need to give Trude an extensive Jewish education. At her own insistence, Trude studied Talmud, Hebrew language, and cultural Zionism. She also received an excellent secular education, obtaining a doctorate in Semitics (the archeology and cultures of the ancient Near East).

When she arrived in the United States, together with her husband, Aaron Rosmarin, Trude planned to teach in a university, but in 1931 it was almost impossible for a woman to get an academic appointment. Instead, with the help of Hadassah, she founded the School of the Jewish Woman in New York. There, Jewish women had the opportunity to study Hebrew language and Jewish history and customs.

Weiss-Rosmarin also started a magazine called *The Jewish Spectator*. First published as a newsletter for the school, it remained in existence long after the school closed. *The Jewish Spectator* developed into an influential journal dealing with important political issues of the day. Weiss-Rosmarin edited the journal for forty years, supporting its publication with a successful speaking and lecturing career. Her editorials and essays were filled with references to talmudic and midrashic texts. She confronted every major issue of the day relating to Jewish survival. *The Jewish Spectator* continued regular publication even after Weiss-Rosmarin's death in 1989.

Marie Syrkin was another exceptional example of an intellectual Jewish woman. She was educated in the early years of the twentieth century and her work was deeply affected by her Jewish interests. Born in Switzerland in 1899, Marie came to the United States with her family in 1908 and attended American schools.

The daughter of a prominent Zionist leader, Marie was well educated in secular and Jewish subjects. She became equally renowned as a writer, a poet, and a translator. She also edited *The Jewish Frontier*, the magazine of the Labor Zionist Movement in America.

Her most famous work, *Blessed is the Match*, is a study of Jewish resistance movements under the Nazis. In 1955, she wrote a biography of her good friend Golda Meir. Syrkin taught English at Brandeis University from 1951 to 1966. She remained active as a writer until her death in 1989.

Two other notable women scholars were Lucy Dawidowicz and Hannah Arendt. Dawidowicz earned her scholarly reputation as a historian of the Holocaust. She wrote *The War Against the Jews* and *A Holocaust Reader*. Her book *The Golden Tradition* recorded the cultural diversity of Jewish life in Eastern Europe before the Holocaust. Dawidowicz died in 1990.

Hannah Arendt, born in 1906 and educated in Germany, became a political and social philosopher. After fleeing Hitler's Germany she worked for Jewish organizations in Paris. In 1941 she escaped to the United States.

After some time, she became a professor at the University of Chicago and then at the New School for Social Research in New York. She was best known for her controversial analysis of anti-Semitism and Nazism. Even after her death in 1975, Arendt's ideas and theories have continued to excite discussion.

As the century continued, Jewish institutions and Jewish studies became better established in North America. A few women with personal or family wealth committed their energy and contributed substantial sums of money to Jewish causes. Such women leaders as Sadie Bronfman, Peggy Tishman, and Shoshana Cardin developed skills that they used on behalf of the expanding needs of Jewish organizations.

A parallel development was the growth of Jewish studies in colleges and universities. Increasing numbers of Jewish scholars were being born and educated in the United States and Canada. At the same time, the feminist movement spread across North America, Europe, and Israel. Together, these two factors influenced Jewish life and Jewish women.

By the late 1960s, some girls in American yeshivot and day schools were demanding and receiving an education in Talmud and legal commentary along with the boys. In the 1980s, advanced yeshivot, organized exclusively for women, were a reality in Israel, too. While a few of these women students entered the American rabbinical seminaries or cantorial schools, many continued their studies in other areas. They became experts in Bible, philosophy, literature, law, and music and used their knowledge of Judaism to enhance those fields.

The spread of Jewish scholarship among women has brought fresh perspectives to many aspects of Jewish life. Today, an increasing number of women are able to speak with authority and present their views on the issues that interest them most. Their example is attracting more women into areas of learning once studied only by men.

Judith Kaplan Eisenstein

Judith Kaplan was born in 1909 into a privileged position in Jewish life. Her father, Rabbi Mordecai Kaplan, was a learned and observant Jew who taught at the Conservative Jewish Theological Seminary in New York.

A very bright child, Judy was reading before she was three years old and began to learn Hebrew at four. The oldest of four daughters, she was always very close to her father. She constantly asked him questions about Jewish practices and their meaning and learned about Judaism by living it.

Judith went to Hebrew school at the Jewish Center where her father was the rabbi. There she studied Hebrew, Jewish history and customs, and even some of Rashi's commentaries.

As he grew older, Rabbi Mordecai Kaplan began to feel that American Jews needed a different outlook on Judaism. A new philosophy would make the old traditions more meaningful to them. With that in mind, he organized the Society for the Advancement of Judaism in 1922. It began as one small congregation with Rabbi Kaplan as its leader.

One of Rabbi Kaplan's beliefs was that men and women should be equal within Judaism. To demonstrate that belief, he arranged for Judy to be called up to the *bimah*, the platform where the rabbi stands and from which the Torah is read.

Judith Kaplan was the first American Jewish girl to publicly become a Bat Mitzvah. At a Saturday morning service she recited the traditional blessings and then read a portion of the Torah in Hebrew and English as well as the *haftorah*. As she later recalled: "no thunder sounded, no lightning struck and the rest of the day was all rejoicing."

By the time Judith finished high school, she was steeped in Judaism, but her particular interest was music. She had been studying music from the time she was seven years old, going regularly to the Institute of Musical Art (later renamed the Julliard School of Music).

At the Teachers College of Columbia University, where she received a B.A. and a master's degree, Judith specialized in music education. At the same time, she took courses at the Teacher's Institute of the Jewish Theological Seminary.

In June 1934, Judith married her father's assistant and disciple, Rabbi Ira Eisenstein. Ira had fallen in love with Judith the first time he saw her. Several years after they met, the two worked together on a musical play. By the time the play was produced, Judith and Ira had become a couple. The marriage was a long and happy one and the Eisensteins wrote many other musical productions together.

Ira was committed to a reconstructed Judaism and had been working with Mordecai Kaplan for several years. After his marriage he became even closer to the Kaplan family. He worked with Rabbi Kaplan on a magazine called *The Reconstructionist*. Its aim was to introduce Jews to the new ideas of the Society for the Advancement of Judaism and make Jewish life more meaningful for contemporary Jews.

Two years after Judith and Ira's marriage, their son Ethan was born. Sadly, the child had severe developmental problems. The young parents made the painful decision to place him in a special institution. Their daughter Miriam Rachel was born in 1938. Seven years later, they had another daughter, Ann Nehama.

In the Eisenstein household the traditions of Sabbath and festivals were followed with joy and singing. *Seders* in Judith and Ira's home were enriched with songs in different languages and from different musical traditions, "sung out lustily and appreciatively."

During those years Judith Eisenstein also maintained a teaching career. From 1929 to 1954, she taught music at the Teacher's Institute and the College of Jewish Studies at the Jewish Theological Seminary. She also wrote many articles and published collections of songs.

In 1954, the Eisenstein family moved to Chicago where Ira had his own congregation. While there, Judith taught at the Chicago College of Jewish Studies.

Judith and Ira missed their old home and the Kaplan family. After five years, they moved back to New York and Ira again worked with the Society for the Advancement of Judaism.

The Society was becoming a movement. More and more congregations wanted to be part of it and to adopt its rituals and philosophy. Plans were made for a rabbinical seminary in Philadelphia to train Jews as Reconstructionist rabbis.

Judith continued her work in music, teaching, and writing. In 1966, she earned a Ph.D. in Jewish music from the Hebrew Union College (the Reform Jewish Seminary in New York). After receiving her advanced degree, she remained there to teach cantors at the School of Sacred Music. By then, Judith Kaplan Eisenstein had published three collections of Jewish music and written five cantatas together with Ira.

Judith Kaplan Eisenstein (right) was the first American Jewish girl to publicly become a Bat Mitzvah.

When Rabbi Ira Eisenstein was invited to act as part-time rabbi for a small congregation, the couple traveled out to the north shore of Long Island every other week. For the twelve years that Ira was rabbi, Judith was an active member and led congregational singing. From time to time she gave lectures on Jewish music.

Judith and Ira were much loved and admired by the members of the Reconstructionist Synagogue of the north shore. They continued their relationship with the congregation long after their retirement.

Professor Nehama Leibowitz, a famous and beloved figure among Bible students in Israel.

Heritage of Music, Judith's most scholarly work, was published in 1972. It surveys the music of the Jewish people from ancient times to the present. Actual songs from all parts of the world are included.

Judith retired in 1979 when she was seventy years old, but continued to write articles on Jewish music. In Woodstock, New York, where they lived, Ira and Judith organized a new Reconstructionist *havurah*. Well past retirement, Judith Kaplan Eisenstein continued to share the love of Judaism that influenced her own life. She died in February 1996.

Nehama Leibowitz

Nehama Leibowitz has inspired women for decades. Even at the age of ninety, she continues to be one of the most respected biblical scholars in Israel and is considered a great Bible teacher throughout the world.

Nehama, born in Riga, Latvia in 1905, was educated in Germany. At home, her parents maintained Jewish traditions and spoke Hebrew to their children. She and her brother Yehoshua were educated equally in Bible and Talmud but Nehama loved Bible studies best.

In 1930, Nehama and her husband moved from Berlin to Palestine. Safe from the horrors of Hitler and the growing anti-Semitism in Germany, she began the work she loved. Until 1955, Leibowitz taught at the Mizrachi Women Teacher's Seminary in Jerusalem and gave weekly Bible lessons over the radio.

Not only did Nehama discuss and explain the biblical passages, she also examined and compared the opinions of the sages on each passage. What did Rashi say? How did Maimonides disagree and why? Using this question and answer technique, Nehama would extract the religious or moral principle.

By 1957, Leibowitz had won the Israel Prize for Education and was teaching at Tel Aviv University where she became a professor in 1968. During those years she recorded her explanations of the *sidra* of the week, the biblical portion read every week in the synagogue. These "studies" were eventually assembled into books and translated from Hebrew into other languages. In addition to *Studies in the Weekly Sidra*, Leibowitz published studies explaining each of the five books of the Torah, which have been translated into English.

Professor Leibowitz, with her brown suit and beret, was a beloved and familiar figure on Israeli campuses. A pathfinder and a popularizer of Bible, her teaching methods are a model wherever the Hebrew Bible is studied. Her commentaries are used by the World Zionist Organization for the study of Torah in Jewish communities all over the world. Even after her official retirement, she continued teaching Torah for its own sake, to students who came to her home for seminars. Today, women scholars, inspired by her spirituality, are following in her footsteps.

Cynthia Ozick

As opportunities for secular and Jewish education increased, many Jewish women entered the world of literature. They became writers of poetry, fiction, and essays. They wrote in Hebrew and Yiddish as well as all the languages of Europe and America. It would be possible to devote an entire book just to Jewish women authors without naming them all. In America, however, Cynthia Ozick stands above the rest.

Cynthia Ozick is one of the most brilliant and respected authors of late twentieth century America. She has succeeded in combining an understanding of Jewish life, law, and philosophy with her literary talent. Ozick's novels, essays, and stories introduce her readers to an array of Jewish characters and life styles.

Born in New York City in 1928, Cynthia always knew she would be a writer. When asked about her childhood in the Bronx, she recalled a neighborhood where anti-Semitism was

Cynthia Ozick is

one of the outstanding

American writers

of the twentieth century.

common and reading was not. A traveling library stopped regularly at her father's drugstore and she was allowed to borrow two books each week. From this experience, she developed a love of books and reading that would last all her life.

Cynthia was sent to *Heder* (an Orthodox Hebrew school) but was never inspired by the old-fashioned teaching methods. She got most of her Jewish education informally, from those around her, and from independent reading. Cynthia's maternal grandmother was a strong influence on her. Grandmother read to her and told stories of her own early years.

In a later interview, Cynthia described herself as "a luckless goose girl." She recalled being "cross-eyed, dumb, an imbecile in arithmetic."

Despite those painful beginnings, Cynthia went to Hunter College High School and New York University where she graduated with honors. One year later, she received an M.A. in English from Ohio State University.

Cynthia's first job, in 1950, was as a copywriter, writing ads for a Boston department store. Almost simultaneously, she began publishing articles and working on a first novel.

In 1952, Cynthia married Bernard Hallote, a lawyer. The couple had a daughter, Rachel Sarah. By 1964 the young mother was back at work in New York, teaching English at New York University.

Cynthia's first novel, *Trust*, was published two years later. It was praised as a "*tour de force*," filled with symbolism and "keen satire." Short story collections, essays, and poems followed. Many of her works concern the post-war generation of American Jews and their efforts to make sense of the Holocaust. Her characters are often involved in a search for meaning. They struggle with the tension between Jewish mystical ideas and the material world.

When the women's movement became a force in American Jewish life, Ozick turned her analytic mind to the problems of Jewish feminism. Her brilliant essay "Notes Toward Finding the Right Question (A Vindication of the Rights of Jewish Women)" was published in *Lilith*, the Jewish women's magazine, in 1979. It became a guide for many Jewish women seeking to harmonize feminism and Judaism.

Cynthia lives in New Rochelle, New York with her husband. She still loves books and considers herself "a compulsive reader." She told an interviewer that she "writes late into the night and gets up at noon." She does most of the cooking for herself and her husband but admitted: "I burn the food a lot."

Ozick's story, "The Shawl," which relates a woman's experience during the Holocaust, won the O. Henry Award for the best short story of 1981. Ozick later rewrote "The Shawl" as a play.

Cynthia Ozick has won many awards and much recognition and respect from the American literary community. One prize, the Mildred and Harold Strauss Living Award, sponsored by the National Institute of Arts and Letters, gave Ozick a yearly stipend for a minimum of five years beginning in 1983. It allowed her to concentrate on her writing without having to teach or lecture.

Cynthia Ozick's skill at storytelling, her keen interest in the many aspects of Jewish life, and her brilliant mind have established her as one of the most exceptional writers of her generation.

Judith Hauptman

Judith Hauptman never planned to be a pioneer or a role model. As a student at Yeshiva of Flatbush, Brooklyn, in the early 1960s, she excelled in all her studies. When the girls in her tenth grade class were told they would no longer have Talmud classes, she did not protest. Judith simply assumed that was the way it had to be. After five years of studying with their male classmates, the girls were assigned to typing classes. The boys moved on to more advanced studies in Talmud.

Judith continued to be a fine student. She earned a B.A. from Barnard College and a B.H.L. (Bachelor of Hebrew Letters) at the nearby Jewish Theological Seminary. Here she was reintroduced to Talmud.

Because of her skill in reading and understanding the Aramaic texts, she would occasionally substitute when the professor was absent. At graduation in 1967, Judith was offered a position teaching Talmud at the Jewish Theological Seminary's part-time Hebrew High School.

Almost without planning, Judith's life began to shape itself around her interest and expertise in Talmud. While teaching, she earned a master's degree from the seminary. Then in 1972, Hauptman received an invitation that would introduce her to the world of Jewish feminism.

A small number of women had formed a group that they called *Ezrat Nashim* (the Women's Gallery). They wanted to convince the Conservative Jewish leadership that women should be included as equals in all religious rituals.

The Conservative movement had ruled, in 1955, that women could be called up to recite the blessing on the Torah. However, few people knew about this ruling. Even fewer rabbis permitted the practice in their synagogues.

The women of *Ezrat Nashim* wanted to remind rabbis that this was already allowed. They also wished to introduce some new ideas. Women should be counted in the minyan of ten required to begin communal prayers. Women ought to be permitted to read from the Torah and to become rabbis and cantors. Lacking fundamental knowledge of the talmudic texts that dealt with these issues, the group needed a skilled teacher.

Three members of *Ezrat Nashim* knew Judith Hauptman and invited her into the group. Each week she brought a Talmud text to be analyzed. The women learned about Jewish law, and Judith absorbed the ideas of Jewish feminism. "They raised my consciousness," said Judith of her year-long involvement with *Ezrat Nashim*.

By the summer of 1973, the group was ready. Uninvited, they approached the convention of Conservative rabbis, stood up at the general meeting, and listed their demands. Although the initial reaction was shock, the women ultimately achieved their goals.

The law committee of the Conservative rabbinical assembly ruled in favor of counting women in a minyan and accepted most of the women's demands as legally valid. However, they allowed each congregation and rabbi to decide these issues on an individual basis. They also agreed to form a committee to investigate the possibility of ordaining women as rabbis.

When they did, Judith was one of the few scholars asked to submit a legal opinion. Although her opinion was not published for several years, the committee was aware of her arguments.

In 1974, while still working for her Ph.D., Judith married Milton Adesnik, a biologist and professor at New York University Medical School. After many years of study, she received her doctorate in 1982 and became the first female professor of Talmud at the Jewish Theological Seminary.

Commenting on her teaching goals, Dr. Hauptman explained: "I try to get people excited about Talmud and about the practice of Judaism." With three teenage sons, Judith Hauptman is a role model for both young men and young women.

Dr. Judith Hauptman,

the first female professor of Talmud

at the Jewish Theological Seminary of America.

The Women's Tefilah Group of Great Neck, New York wore costumes to the reading of the megillah at Purim.

Chapter 20

Women and Jewish Spirituality

With so many Jewish women finding fulfillment and equality in the work place and in the academic world, those who were more observant of Jewish law and traditions began to push for religious change. They wanted equality in Jewish ritual as well.

To some women, equality meant they would have the right to be members of synagogues independently of their husbands. They would be able to hold office and share in decision making. For others it meant the right to be called for the honor of blessing or holding the Torah.

Many women wanted equal education for girls. They believed their daughters should have Bat Mitzvah ceremonies equivalent to the Bar Mitzvah ceremonies their sons had. Some adult women sought the Jewish education they had been denied as children.

These ideas began as tentative requests in the 1950s and 1960s. However, as Jewish women became more educated and gained support from men, the requests became firmer and more specific. Some women began asking: "Why can't we be spiritual leaders like men?"

Women leaders of congregations were not unheard of, even before the twentieth century. Hannah Rachel Werbermacher preached sermons in her own *schul* in Ludomir, Poland. Lily Montagu was a lay preacher in London.

In the early 1900s, Regina Jonas, a German Jewish woman, studied at a Reform Seminary for rabbis in Berlin. Although the school stopped short of granting her a rabbinical degree, she did receive ordination privately from another rabbi.

In the United States, the first Jewish woman to preach from a pulpit was Ray Frank. She worked as a reporter and correspondent for a few San Francisco newspapers. While in Spokane, Washington just before Rosh Hashana (the New Year) in 1890, Frank learned that this small Jewish community had no service scheduled. She set about organizing one and offered to preach.

Ray Frank's sermons, delivered on the two days of the New Year and on Yom Kippur, impressed many Jews. From that time on, she was invited to give sermons throughout the American Northwest and was often called the "lady rabbi." When she married in 1901, she stopped preaching and settled down to a more traditional life with her husband.

In Meridian, Mississippi, Paula Ackerman, widow of a beloved rabbi, was asked to assume her husband's role after he died in 1950. She served for almost three years. Not only did Ackerman lead services, give sermons, and teach, she also officiated at weddings, funerals, and conversions.

Although these women were sometimes considered rabbis, no woman was officially ordained by a rabbinical seminary until 1972.

That was the year Sally Preisand became a rabbi.

Rabbi Sally Preisand

at her ordination in 1972.

Sally Preisand

One of four children, Sally was born in 1946 in Cleveland, Ohio. Her Reform Jewish parents had raised her and her sister to believe they could be anything they wanted, just as their two brothers could. Sally never questioned that belief. It sustained her through many challenges and helped her become a pioneer in the Jewish world.

While she was growing up, Sally Preisand wanted to be a teacher. When her favorite subject was English, she planned to be an English teacher. When it was history, she said she would be a history teacher.

By the time she reached her teen years, Sally's favorite subject changed once more. She loved the study of Judaism best. What better way to teach Judaism than to become a rabbi?

Sally had already served as chaplain of her youth group, leading services and assisting the rabbi. She loved it. By the time she was sixteen, she had made her decision. She would study to be a Reform rabbi.

The continued doubts, even the laughter of others, did not deter Sally. Many assumed that she really wanted to marry a rabbi, not to be one. Sally did not allow the feelings of others to discourage her, though. She earned a B.A. in English from the University of Cincinnati in 1968. Immediately afterwards, she took a degree in Hebrew literature from Hebrew Union College, the Reform Jewish Seminary in Cincinnati. Next came her rabbinic internship.

At last, in 1972, Sally Preisand, the only woman among her classmates, was officially ordained. At twenty-six, she became the first woman rabbi in the United States.

Rabbi Sally Preisand's first post was as assistant rabbi at the Stephen Wise Free Synagogue in New York City. When it was time to move on to her own pulpit, she encountered problems and rejections.

Preisand did not give up. During those difficult years while she searched for a job, Sally wrote a book, *Judaism and the New Woman*. She also accepted invitations to speak all around the country. "I wanted people to see that I was human, and that it was not such a ridiculous idea for a woman to be a rabbi," she explained.

Finally, Sally Preisand found a congregation of her own. Since 1981, Rabbi Preisand has served as rabbi of Monmouth Reform Temple in Tinton Falls, New Jersey. Her ultimate goal, she says, is for people "to see the rabbi as a rabbi, and not as a man or a woman."

Sandy Eisenberg Sasso

As of June 1994, the Reconstructionist Movement had graduated and ordained sixty-two women rabbis. Sandy Eisenberg Sasso was the first. She decided to become a rabbi in 1963. That was four years before a Reconstructionist seminary even existed, and nine years before Sally Preisand was ordained as the first woman rabbi.

Sandy Eisenberg was born in Philadelphia in 1947. Her father came from an Orthodox background; her mother's family was not religious at all. Her parents were committed to Zionism and to many other struggles for justice that Jews often supported. The Eisenberg home reflected a mixture of traditions.

Girls were not customarily educated for Bat Mitzvah in the Reform Temple that Sandy's family joined. Instead, boys and girls were confirmed together when they were sixteen.

Sandy liked Hebrew school. The head rabbi, Bertram Korn, was a wonderful teacher and a great inspiration. She looked forward to the confirmation ceremony and her chance to participate in the service.

Sandy still remembers that ceremony as a "powerful experience." The students' families crowded the sanctuary, proud of their sons and daughters. There were 120 students being con-firmed and each one had a part to read in the service. They wore white robes, and the girls carried roses and small white Bibles.

After her confirmation, Sandy made a choice that would radically affect her life. She told Rabbi Korn and her parents that she wanted to become a rabbi. Outside her most intimate cir-cle, however, no one suspected her secret dream. Sandy didn't want to say anything that would make her seem different or set her apart from her friends.

Following high school, Sandy remained close to home, enrolling in nearby Temple University. She majored in religion and took courses in Hebrew, but she began to rethink her early decision.

Did she really want to be a rabbi? Sandy asked herself. Was it realistic? In the mid-1960s there were no women rabbis, and Sally Preisand was not yet enrolled at the Hebrew Union College. Even if Sandy was ordained, could she ever get a job as a rabbi? All these doubts pur-sued her through her college years. Then, when Sandy was a senior, her synagogue asked her to write and lead a creative worship service. Sandy accepted. She brought in modern readings and poetry and wove them between the traditional prayers.

The congregation loved it, but more important, Sandy loved it. Once again, her old idea of becoming a rabbi was confirmed.

Rabbi Korn suggested she apply to the new Reconstructionist Rabbinical College. It had just opened in Philadelphia, right beside Temple University. The college philosophy suited her, and they were happy to accept a woman.

There were fewer than a dozen candidates for the rabbinical degree — Sandy Eisenberg was the only woman. As an "insurance policy" she also took courses at Temple University toward her master's degree in religion.

Even in a school as progressive and open to women as the Reconstructionist Rabbinical College, Sandy did not always feel accepted. There were negative comments from other Jews, and she learned that Jewish law excluded women from many of its rituals and its rulings. As she began to study rabbinic texts, Sandy realized that they totally excluded women's voices and perceptions. "The place where I thought I belonged didn't include me," she said.

Nevertheless, Sandy kept going. She learned much about Judaism and about being a rabbi.

Sandy also met her husband, Dennis Sasso, at the seminary. The two were married at the end of their first year. As she marched down the aisle in her wedding dress, Sandy held the same small white Bible she had carried for her confirmation.

In 1974, both Sandy and Dennis were ordained. Sandy was the first, and only, woman to become a rabbi in the Reconstructionist Movement that year.

After graduation, Rabbi Sandy Sasso found work at the Manhattan Reconstructionist Havurah. Dennis took over the leadership of the North Shore Congregation, which had been led by Ira and Judith Eisenstein (see Chapter 19). After a few years, Sandy and Dennis had their first child, David.

Now that they were a family, the Sassos felt they wanted to be together. As leaders of separate congregations they had to be apart on Sabbaths and holidays. In addition, Sandy now needed a part-time position so she could spend more time with her son.

At this time, Congregation Beth-El Tzedek of Indianapolis, Indiana was searching for a new rabbi. Dennis went to interview for the job. He was told that if he accepted the post, one of his duties would be to hire a second rabbi to help him.

As a rabbi, Sandy Eisenberg Sasso enjoys the chance to share her ideas with others.

This seemed the perfect opportunity for the Sassos. After an interview with Sandy, the couple were welcomed at the Indianapolis congregation. They became the first husband-wife team to serve as rabbis. Within a short time, their second child, Debora, was born.

Rabbi Sandy Sasso has shared the pulpit at Beth-El Tzedek with her husband for over eighteen years. She and Dennis make equal contributions to the Temple and take turns delivering sermons. They both teach and tend to pastoral duties for their congregants. In addition to her work as a rabbi, Sandy Sasso has written articles and books. She maintains that women can bring a different perspective to traditional Jewish ideas and forms. "Because women have been excluded from leadership roles for so long," she says, "we need to fill in that empty space." Today, "women are giving voice to concerns and issues that have never been addressed before."

Always conscious of what she calls "that absent voice" of women, Sandy and her husband Dennis wrote a birth ceremony for a girl while attending rabbinical school. Their ceremony brings a baby girl into the covenant with God just as the circumcision ceremony does for baby boys. Today the "covenantal ceremony" for newborn girls is widely available and is fast becoming a tradition with many young Jewish families.

One of the things Rabbi Sandy Sasso most enjoys about her job is the opportunity to share her ideas with others. She is also happy to be a role model. "When I hear about women who decided to enter the rabbinate because they saw other women in those roles, I feel I've accomplished something," she says. "I'm pleased that I have been able to open some doors for women in Judaism, in ritual and ceremony, in language and prayer, in reclaiming women's stories and names."

Amy Eilberg

Becoming a rabbi was not easy for Amy Eilberg. She was born in 1954 in Philadelphia and grew up as a Conservative Jew.

After graduation from high school in 1972, Amy went to Brandeis University and majored in Jewish studies. While at Brandeis she became active in Hillel, the Jewish student's campus organization. There she met and became friends with Rabbi Axelrod, the Hillel director.

One Saturday morning, Rabbi Axelrod listened while Amy conducted *shaharit*, the Sabbath morning prayer service. He found her service so moving that he encouraged her to become a rabbi. At first Amy thought he was crazy. She knew no women rabbis and was well aware that the Conservative movement was not yet ordaining women, but his idea remained with her and gradually began to make more sense.

In 1976, after receiving her degree from Brandeis, Amy enrolled at the Jewish Theological Seminary in New York. By this time, the Reform and Reconstructionist movements had already been ordaining women for several years. It was just a matter of time, she thought, until women would be accepted as rabbis. When it happened she would be there.

Amy began to study Talmud and found that she loved it. She was often the only woman in a class of male rabbinical students. She fantasized about taking all the classes the male students took and then coming to the chancellor and challenging him: "What will you do with me now?" She never did this, however.

In 1974, after a great deal of pressure from women, the Conservative Movement agreed to investigate the possibility of female ordination. Amy understood that Conservative Jews considered Jewish law and tradition to be binding on all Jews. In order to admit women as rabbis, Jewish scholars would have to find justification in the law itself. The decision was taking a long time.

In the meantime, Amy went to study and teach in Israel. She taught Talmud at the seminary's Jerusalem branch and waited for the ruling that would allow her to complete her degree.

After several years of study and discussion, the Conservative Committee on Law and Standards finally came to a conclusion. Most of the experts agreed that according to Jewish law it was indeed permissible for women to be rabbis. The vote was eleven to three.

Despite such an overwhelmingly favorable vote, the faculty of the Jewish Theological Seminary decided to postpone the decision

Rabbi Amy Eilberg waited a long time before she was allowed

to be ordained as a Conservative rabbi.

to admit women. Amy was bitterly disappointed. It would be ten more years, she thought, before the question of women rabbis would be considered again. She looked around for other choices.

Perhaps she would get a Ph.D. in Talmud. If she couldn't be a rabbi, then she would teach rabbis. She continued her studies. In 1982, however, she realized that she did not want to work in an academic setting. She wanted to work with people in a more individual way. Amy's father had been a congressman. He had many years of active public service behind him. Her mother held a master's degree in social work and had followed a career of her own, helping people in the community. Amy would do the same.

She left the seminary and enrolled in the social work program at Smith College. After two years, she received her master's degree. As she was preparing to graduate in May 1984, the news broke. The Jewish Theological Seminary had decided to accept women as rabbinical students and would ordain them as rabbis.

That September, Amy Eilberg enrolled once again in the seminary. She had already taken almost all the courses she needed. In June 1985, she became the first woman to be ordained as a Conservative Rabbi.

Now Amy had to decide what kind of rabbinical work she would do. Her first job was as a chaplain in an acute care hospital in Indianapolis. She worked there for three years and found it very rewarding. However, she wanted to work with a congregation. With an offer from a Conservative Synagogue in Philadelphia, she moved back to her hometown and became a pulpit rabbi — a rabbi who is the leader of a specific congregation.

"But I missed the experience of caring for the sick," Rabbi Eilberg recalled. After only one year she returned to her work as a hospital chaplain and realized that this work was her calling. When she moved to San Francisco, Eilberg continued the same kind of work at Stanford University Hospital. Her pastoral duties included counseling the sick and the dying and listening to their fears and worries. She also comforted them and their families through prayer.

Amy felt that there should be a special institution to offer spiritual care to Jewish patients. She wanted to "try and bring the Jewish peace of hospice care" to Jews. A hospice is a place where terminally ill patients can go to die.

Amy began working with a new organization called The Bay Area Jewish Healing Center. The center has no separate hospice building; a chaplain from the center visits either the patient's home or one of the hospitals in the area. The Healing Center had always offered pastoral services to Jewish patients who were ill. Rabbi Eilberg added a special religious service for terminally ill hospice patients.

Although this work sounds very sad, Rabbi Amy Eilberg insists, "It is a tremendous satisfaction and blessing. God sent me to it."

Amy considers her establishment of spiritual care for Jewish hospice patients to be a major achievement in her life, but her finest achievement, she says, is "being a good mother." Amy Eilberg, now divorced, has a young daughter who brings her great joy.

Some women rabbis assert that being a rabbi is not about being a man or a woman. Every rabbi is unique, they say. Each of us offers his or her own contribution to Judaism and Jewish spirituality.

Rabbi Eilberg does not agree. "What is unique about me as a rabbi," she says, "has everything to do with my being a woman." She feels that as a woman and a mother she can communicate her faith in a way that male rabbis do not.

Since Rabbi Amy Eilberg's ordination in 1985, many other Conservative Jewish women have followed her example. In 1991, the Women's League for Conservative Judaism began building a national corps of women Torah readers and religious prayer leaders. The members of the League feel this will help increase the role of women in Conservative synagogue rituals.

WOMEN RABBIS
AND ORTHODOX JEWS

Most Orthodox Jews are still resisting the idea of women rabbis in Jewish life. Blu Greenberg, an Orthodox feminist leader from New York, has stated that America's most traditional group of Jews will eventually accept women as rabbis. Others disagree. Even as the controversy rages, however, change is reaching the staunchest upholders of old traditions.

Often without encouragement from their rabbis, Orthodox women are claiming their own spiritual life. They are flocking to women's schools to study the traditional Jewish texts. They are becoming experts in Talmud and teaching other Jewish women what they have learned. They are learning how to represent other women before the religious court in Israel.

A growing number of observant women are no longer satisfied merely to watch men perform the rituals. In the larger Jewish communities in the United States, they are forming prayer (tefilah) groups. While carefully avoiding the recitation of prayers that require a minyan of men, these groups give women an opportunity to conduct a service. They can read aloud from the Torah and practice the skills involved in leading prayers. In this way they experience the spirituality that is created by group prayer and ritual, an experience once reserved for men alone.

In 1991, the Israeli rabbinate was confronted by the Women of the Wall. For the first time, these rabbis were forced to deal with the right of women to assemble and pray together as a group at the Western Wall *(Kotel)* in Jerusalem.

The Women of the Wall is a mixed group of women, both Orthodox and liberal. They want to be allowed to pray together with a Torah on the women's side of the Western Wall. For praying in this way, they have been stoned and reviled by other Jews.

Some Orthodox rabbis have taken legal steps to prevent groups of women from praying in an organized fashion. The women themselves appealed the decision to the Israeli Supreme Court.

Before ruling, the court appointed a committee for further investigation. The committee is still considering this issue. Jewish women such as Rivka Haut of the United States and Norma Baumel Joseph of Canada are among the women committed to traditional Judaism who have been in the forefront of this struggle. With many other Orthodox Jewish women, they are seeking to be included in more of the spiritual aspects of Jewish life while remaining within the community of traditional Judaism.

The Next Step

As we approach the end of the twentieth century, Jewish women have achieved things our foremothers could not have dreamed. Through commitment, hard work, and vision they are changing the Jewish community and the world.

Sometimes separately, sometimes together, Jewish women of all ages are moving toward a future filled with promise and possibilities. With their accomplishments, they are clearing a path for new generations.

They are paving the way for you.

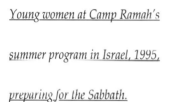

Young women at Camp Ramah's summer program in Israel, 1995, preparing for the Sabbath.

Glossary

abolitionist:
: A person who was against slavery in the United States and worked to abolish it.

aliyah:
: A Hebrew word meaning immigration to Israel, from the root verb *aleh,* "to go up." It is also used when a person is called up for an honor during the Torah service.

anarchist:
: A person who is against all forms of government.

angel:
: A messenger of God. A supernatural being, often in human form, who comes to earth to help an individual or group, or to do God's will.

antibodies:
: Proteins produced in the body that help fight diseases.

Apocrypha:
: A group of fourteen books written in ancient times, but not included in the Bible. Some of these books are based on historical facts as are the three books of the Maccabees. Others are historical novels or traditional stories revolving around biblical characters.

Ashkenazim:
: Jewish people who trace their ancestry back to German origins. The Hebrew word for Germany is *Ashkenaz.*

assimilation:
: The process by which people accept the customs and lifestyle of the majority community and gradually abandon their own distinctive customs and lifestyles.

Assyrian:
: People originating from the ancient land of Assyria, north of Israel.

Auschwitz:
: A concentration camp in Poland where Jews were sent to be killed by the Nazi government of Germany during World War II.

autobiography:
: An account of a person's life written by herself or himself.

Baal Shem Tov:
: The nickname of Israel ben Eliezer, the founder of the Hasidic Movement, which began in Poland in the 1700s. The name means "master of a good name."

bankruptcy: A situation in which a person, group of persons, or business is judged by a court to owe more money than he, she, or it can pay.

Bar Mitzvah: A rite of passage for a Jewish boy at the age of thirteen. The words literally mean "son of the commandment" and imply that the boy now has the responsibilities of an adult Jew.

Bat Mitzvah: A rite of passage for a Jewish girl between the ages of twelve and thirteen. The words mean "daughter of the commandment." This ceremony marking a girl's adult status in the community is relatively new in the United States. Recently, the practice has started to spread to Jewish communities in other parts of the world.

B.C.E./C.E.:   An abbreviation used by Jews meaning the years before the common era or before the year of the birth of Jesus. Christians renumber the years and centuries beginning with that year, referring to them as A.D. (*anno Domini,* "in the year of our Lord"). Jews prefer C.E. (common era). Jews also have their own calendar and system of counting, beginning with creation. The year 1996 corresponds to the Jewish year 5756/5757.

Berber: A member of a North African tribal culture that has existed from the first century of the common era.

bimah: The Hebrew word for the platform from which the Torah is read.

blessing: A prayer recited for a specific act or event, or to bless a person.

boycott: The refusal to deal with or buy from a person or group of persons as a means of changing their behavior.

Canaan: The name for Palestine before it was inhabited by the ancient Israelites.

cantor: The synagogue official who sings the prayers in front of the congregation.

challah: A special kind of bread made with eggs and usually braided; traditionally served as part of the Sabbath meal.

Conservative: A person who is inclined to preserve existing conditions or institutions. Conservative Judaism tries to maintain tradition while adapting it to modern times.

contraceptive: A device used to prevent women from becoming pregnant.

Crusade: A military expedition of European Christians during the Middle Ages organized for the purpose of taking Palestine from the Arabs.

dowry: Money, land, or other property given to a woman by her family at the time of her marriage.

emancipation: The act of freeing a person or a group of people or granting them rights previously denied, or both.

Enlightenment: A period during the eighteenth and nineteenth centuries which emphasized intellectual and spiritual development. This new emphasis began in the Christian communities of Europe and spread to the Jewish communities.

eretz: The Hebrew word for land. *Eretz Israel* means "the land of Israel."

exemption: Freedom from an obligation to which others are subject.

exile: A prolonged, usually forced, separation from one's country or community.

Falashas: The name given to the Jews of Ethiopia by the Ethiopian non-Jews.

firzogerin: A Yiddish title for the woman who led the prayer service in the women's section of the synagogue, alternatively called a *zogerke.* She was usually the most learned woman in the community.

Galilee: An area of northern Israel where many of the early Zionist settlements were established.

Geniza: A storeroom for preserving documents and books. Jews maintained such storerooms for documents, books, and letters that could not be thrown away because they contained the name of God. The most famous *Geniza* was located in the Ibn Ezra Synagogue in the ancient city of Fostat, Egypt, now part of Cairo.

ghetto: A section of a city set aside for Jews to live apart from other inhabitants. The word comes from the Italian *ghetto,* which means "iron foundry." The first ghetto, set aside for the Jews of Venice early in the sixteenth century, was located next to an iron foundry.

guardian:	A person legally entrusted with the care of another person or property.
guerrilla:	A member of a small band of soldiers that harasses the enemy by surprise raids.
Hadassah:	The name of a women's service organization with branches all over the world that raises money in support of Israel, especially for medical care.
haftorah (haftarot):	Passage(s) from the biblical books of the Prophets traditionally read each Sabbath in the synagogue after the reading of the Torah.
Hanukkah:	A Jewish holiday commemorating the victory of the Maccabees that ended the persecution of the Jews by their Syrian rulers in the second century B.C.E.
harem:	That part of a Muslim household reserved for women, usually including the wives, mother, and unmarried sisters of the male head of the household.
HaShomer HaTzair:	A Zionist youth organization that operated mainly in eastern Europe. Its members believed that Israel was the homeland of the Jews and that it should be rebuilt and organized according to the principles of socialism.
havurah:	A group of Jews who organize informally for the purposes of study, prayer, or the celebration of Jewish holidays and customs. The word in Hebrew usually refers to a study group.
Heder:	Literally, the Hebrew word for room. However, it was generally used to refer to a room either in a synagogue or in someone's home where young children were taught the beginnings of Jewish education. In the Ashkenazi culture, it eventually came to mean any Hebrew school.
Histadrut:	The General Federation of Labor in Israel, first founded in 1920. It performs many economic, social, and cultural services for its members and has important influence in the Israeli government.
Holocaust:	The term used to refer to the massive destruction of European Jewry by the Nazis and their allies during World War II. Six million Jews were killed.

Holy Land:
A name given by both Christians and Jews to the ancient land of Israel. For Jews, the name signifies the fact that God promised the land to Abraham and his seed forever. For Christians, it is a reminder that Jesus was born and died there. Muslims also regard Israel as a holy land because Jerusalem is where their prophet, Muhammed, ascended to heaven.

Inquisition:
The official investigation into religious heresy organized and run by the Catholic Church from the thirteenth through the sixteenth centuries.

Israelite:
The name given in the Bible to the early Hebrew tribes who first settled the Middle East.

Kaballah:
The Jewish mystical tradition. The central text of Kaballah is the Zohar, a book written in the twelfth century, whose author is unknown. It contains a collection of the mystical and esoteric teachings of Judaism and was very popular in the Middle Ages.

kibbutz:
A voluntary collective settlement in modern Israel where there is no private ownership of money or property (also called *kvutzah* in Hebrew).

kosher/kashrut:
A description for foods that conform to the Jewish dietary laws as they are outlined in the Bible. *Kashrut* is the Hebrew noun for these dietary laws.

Kotel:
The Hebrew word for "wall," usually used to refer to the remainder of the Western Wall of the ancient Temple of Jerusalem. It is used as a gathering place for Jews to worship and pray in modern Israel.

kvutzah:
See **kibbutz.**

Labor Zionist Movement:
A branch of the Zionist Movement that believed in setting up a socialist government for Jews in their ancient homeland. Branches of this organization were active in the United States from 1903 and continue to support the labor party in Israel today.

legend:
A story handed down by tradition. Legends are often accepted as historical fact even though there is no proof of their authenticity.

literary salon:
A gathering of people for the purpose of exchanging ideas and becoming known in literary or artistic circles.

liturgy:	A specific form or order of prayer, accepted by a religious group, usually recited at set times.
Maccabees:	The family of Mattathias and his five sons, Simon, John, Eliezer, Judah, and Jonathan, who first rebelled against the Syrian king and his anti-Jewish policy. The military leader of the group, Judah, was nicknamed *Maccabee*, meaning "the hammer." After the victory of the Jews, descendants of this family ruled Judea for several generations. They are also referred to as the Hasmoneans.
Marrano:	Literally meaning "swine," the name given to a Jew who originated in Spain or Portugal, or in the Spanish or Portuguese colonies, who was forced to convert to Catholicism but practiced Judaism in secret.
massacre:	The killing of large numbers of people.
Megillah (Megillat):	The Hebrew word for scroll. Certain books of the Bible are often referred to as scrolls, especially the books of Ruth and Esther. In Hebrew they are called *Megillat Ruth* and *Megillat Esther*.
melamed:	A teacher of Hebrew, especially for young children. The word stems from the Hebrew *lelamed*, "to teach."
memoirs:	A diary that outlines a person's life, or parts of his or her life.
Messiah:	An expected savior or deliverer. According to Jewish tradition, the Messiah will come and usher in a time of peace and harmony for all people. Christians believe that Jesus Christ was the expected Messiah. Observant Jews are still waiting for the Messiah to come.
Midrash:	A particular kind of rabbinic literature which consists of explanations of the Bible combined with legends and commentary. The word comes from the Hebrew *drash*, which means "to seek" or "to examine."
minyan:	A quorum of ten required to conduct a public worship service. Traditionally, the ten were all men over the age of thirteen. More recently, Reform, Conservative, and Reconstructionist Jews count women and men

in making up the required ten people.

Mishnah: The oral law and teachings of the early sages. This work was compiled and written down in six volumes by Judah HaNasi (the prince) in the second century C.E. It forms the core of the later writings, called the *gemarah*. See **Talmud**.

mitzvot: Commandments.

Muhammed: The religious and political leader of the Arabs in the seventh century C.E. He composed the Koran, the Muslim holy book. After his death, a new religion, Islam, was organized by his followers.

nationalism: Devotion to one's own nation and its interests. Also, a movement for national independence.

Nobel prize: A prestigious international prize given to those considered particularly talented or deserving in a variety of fields, including the sciences, literature, economics, and the advancement of peace. It was originated by Alfred Nobel (1833-1896) of Sweden and is awarded annually in Stockholm.

nomadic: Wandering; usually a group of people with no set home territory, who live by traveling from one area to another to find food for themselves or their animals.

non-conformist: A person who either refuses or is unable to act according to accepted standards.

ordained: Invested officially as a religious leader, usually by a recognized institution or by another person already ordained.

Orthodox: Conforming to traditional religious doctrine. One of the four branches of Judaism.

pagan: A person who is not a member of an organized monotheistic religion. This term usually refers to people who practiced tribal religions in ancient times.

Palestine: The Roman name for the territory that today includes Israel and parts of Jordan and Egypt. It was originally named for the Philistine tribe, which lived on its southwestern coast. The name was used to refer to the ancient land of Israel from Roman times until the establishment of the modern state of Israel in 1948.

Passover: The spring holiday marking the exodus of the Jews from Egypt.

patron: A wealthy person who encourages or supports an artist, a charity, etc.

persecution: The pursuit, harassment, or oppressive treatment of persons or groups because of their race, religion, or belief.

Persia: The old name for modern-day Iran, a country bordering Iraq and Turkey on the west and Afghanistan on the east.

Pharaoh: The official title of the ancient ruler of Egypt.

pogrom: An organized massacre, usually referring to the Russian persecution of Jews and the destruction of their communities.

polonium: A radioactive chemical element.

prophetess: The feminine form of the word prophet. A person who speaks with divine inspiration or foretells the future.

prostitution: The act of engaging in sexual intercourse for money or other payment.

psychoanalysis: A method for treating emotional or mental problems by exploring the unconscious mind.

Rabbinics: The literature of Jewish law, traditions, and methods in their varied forms. It includes prayers, Kaballah, philosophy, Bible, theology, and Hebrew grammar.

radioisotopes: A radioactive combination of chemical elements (isotopes), usually artificially produced.

radium: A highly radioactive metallic element that produces radon and alpha particles. It was discovered by the French-Polish scientist, Madame Marie Curie.

rebbe: The Yiddish word referring to the scholar and spiritual leader of a Jewish community. The word usually refers to Hasidic rabbis.

rebbitzen: The Yiddish word for the wife of a rabbi.

Reconstructionist: One of the four denominations of Judaism recognized in the United States. It was first organized by Rabbi Mordecai Kaplan in the 1920s.

Reform: To change or improve someone or something. It is the name of one of the four branches of modern Judaism, organized in Germany in the early 1800s for the purpose of reforming traditional Judaism.

Renaissance: A period of time from the fourteenth through the seventeenth centuries that was marked by the revival of classical learning and secular art and literature, especially in Italy.

ritual purity *(niddah):* The laws followed by an observant married Jewish woman that involve keeping away from her husband during her menstrual period and bathing in a special ritual bath (mikvah) before resuming sexual relations with him.

Rosh Hodesh: Literally, the "head of the month" or the first day of the month. Rosh Hodesh has often been considered a special holiday for women.

Sabbath: Saturday, the seventh day of the week. According to Jewish tradition, the Sabbath was the day on which God rested from creating the world. In memory of that first rest day, Jews are commanded to refrain from any activity that involves work or creation of any kind.

sacrifice: The offering of something to God as an act of worship. In ancient times, the Israelites sacrificed animals to God in the Temple in Jerusalem.

sanctuary: A holy place or a place providing refuge or safety.

Sanhedrin: The ancient Jewish governing body in Palestine, parallel to a modern Parliament. It was the supreme political, religious, and judicial body of the Jews in Palestine during the Roman period until 425 C.E.

scribe: A person who copies manuscripts.

Scripture: The sacred writings of the Hebrew Bible (*Tanakh*). For Christians, Scripture refers to both the Hebrew Bible (Old Testament) and the New Testament.

seder: The traditional ritual meal conducted on the first and second nights of Passover. During the seder, the story of the exodus of the Israelites from Egypt is retold.

sefer: The Hebrew word for book. When capitalized *Sefer* refers to the Torah.

Sephardim: The Hebrew word for Jews who trace their origins from Spain *(Sepharad)* beginning with the expulsion of Jews from Spain in 1492 and Portugal in 1497.

sexual harassment: The term used to describe unacceptable behavior of men toward women, especially in the workplace. This may include unnecessary touching, sexually explicit language, or suggestions that imply a woman's job status might be improved in return for sexual favors.

Shaharit: The morning service recited daily by observant Jews.

Shavuot: The Feast of Weeks, the Jewish holiday celebrating the harvest of first fruits in Israel. It occurs seven weeks after Passover and is believed to mark the day when the Jews received the Ten Commandments from God at Mount Sinai.

Sh'ma: The Hebrew word for "hear." It is the first word of the Hebrew prayer, "Hear O Israel, the Lord our God is one," which is a quotation from the Hebrew Bible (Deuteronomy 6:4). The Sh'ma prayer proclaims that God is a single entity and is unique. It is traditionally recited during morning and evening prayers and before going to bed at night.

Shomrim: The Hebrew word for guards or watchmen. The *Shomrim* were an organized group of Jewish guards who protected the Zionist pioneers and their fields from attacks by Arabs.

sidra: Aramaic word corresponding to the Hebrew "seder," meaning order. It refers to the weekly portion of the Torah that Jews read in the synagogue on Monday, Thursday, Shabbat, and holidays.

Simhat Torah: "Joy in the Torah." A holiday that celebrates the Jewish people's love of the law (Torah). Simhat Torah is observed annually at the end of the Sukkot holiday, usually in late September or October. Congregations gather to sing and dance with the Torah scrolls and to express their joy with

Torah law and Judaism. The annual Torah cycle is concluded and begun anew.

Socialism: A political philosophy. Socialists believe that all property, including capital, land, and industry, should be owned by the community as a whole and not by private individuals.

soothsayer: A fortuneteller; a person who can predict what will happen in the future.

suffrage (women's): The right to vote. Women who were active in the campaign to win women the right to vote were called Suffragists or Suffragettes.

sultan: The supreme ruler of a Muslim country, equivalent to a king.

synagogue: A Jewish house of worship.

tallit: A prayer shawl traditionally worn by Jewish men, and more recently by some women, during communal prayer. According to biblical specifications, it is required to have fringes at the two ends and special knots at each of the four corners.

Talmud: A collection of commentaries, decisions and traditions based on biblical law, codified in about 500 C.E. The Talmud is made up of the *Mishnah*, the original collection of traditional oral law, and the *Gemarah*, commentaries on the *Mishnah*.

tefilah: Hebrew word for prayer.

tefilin: Phylacteries; small wooden boxes with leather straps attached. The boxes contain copies of the complete Sh'ma prayer, which Jews are required to recite regularly. The observant Jewish male places one of these boxes on his forehead and another on his right arm, conforming to the biblical commandment in the Sh'ma prayer that says: "You shall bind them for a sign upon your hand and they shall be for frontlets between your eyes." *Tefilin* are not used on Shabbat or holidays.

tehines: The Yiddish word for personal prayers, mostly written for women to recite, and usually connected to the specific tasks and traditional duties of Jewish women. The word originates from the Hebrew *tehina* (plural: *tehinot*). Many *tehines* were written by women.

Torah: The Five Books of Moses, the first five books of the Hebrew Bible. These are Genesis, Exodus, Leviticus, Numbers, and Deuteronomy.

tradition: The handing down of beliefs, legends, and customs from one generation to the next, or the specific custom itself, as in "This is a tradition I learned from my mother."

tribes: Groups of related individuals, usually tracing their origins to a common ancestor, who share the same beliefs and customs.

tzaddik: Hebrew word for righteous. Used as a noun, it refers to a person who is both wise and righteous.

tzarist: Pertaining to or believing in the tzar. The tzar was the supreme ruler of Russia until the Revolution in 1917 destroyed the tzarist regime and established a form of socialism.

tzedakah: Hebrew word meaning "righteousness." It has come to mean charity because, according to Jewish law, an act of charity is one of the requirements of a righteous person.

tzitzit: Ritual fringes attached to a small *tallit* that Jewish men are commanded to wear as a constant reminder of God. They are worn by many observant men underneath their regular clothes. Sometimes the fringes are placed outside the clothing so they can be seen.

viceroy: A person appointed to rule a country or a province as the deputy of the king or other supreme ruler.

women's rights movement: The first movement that worked for women's rights was organized in the United States in 1848. It grew throughout the nineteenth century and into the twentieth century. The main goal of this first women's rights movement was to gain the right for women to vote, which was accomplished in 1920. A second movement, to help give women equal opportunity in society, began in 1963.

yeshivah: An academy devoted mainly to the study of Jewish subjects, especially Jewish texts and religious law.

Yiddish: The language of eastern European Jews, beginning in the tenth century.

The base of Yiddish is a dialect of old German. To that base were added words from many different eastern European languages, plus Hebrew words, which took on their own unique pronunciation. The language is usually written in the Hebrew alphabet but has its own rules of spelling and grammar.

Yom Kippur: The Day of Atonement, the holiest and most solemn holiday of the Jewish year. On this day, Jews are required to fast (refrain from eating or drinking) from sunset to sunset in order to atone for their sins.

Zionism: A belief that the Jews are a national group who need a homeland of their own. In the late nineteenth century, Zionism became a political movement that resulted in the establishment of the state of Israel in 1948.

zogerke: See **firzogerin**.

Bibliography

*Ashby, Ruth and Deborah Gore Ohrn, eds. *Herstory: Women Who Changed the World.* New York: Viking Press,1995.

*Bach, Alice and J. Cheryl Axum. *Miriam's Well: Stories About Women in the Bible.* New York: Delacorte Press,1991.

Baskin, Judith, ed. *Jewish Women in Historical Perspective.* Detroit: Wayne State University Press, 1991.

Ben-Zvi, Rachel Yanait. *Before Golda: Manya Shochat.* New York: Biblio Press, 1989.

*Bernstein, Joanne E., and Rose Blue, with Alan Jay Gerber. *Judith Resnick: Challenger Astronaut.* New York: Penguin Books, 1990.

The Bible: The Torah, The Prophets, The Writings. Philadelphia: Jewish Publication Society, 1962–1978.

Birmingham, Stephen. *The Grandees: America's Sephardic Elite.* New York: Harper & Row, 1971.

*Cain, Michael. *Louise Nevelson.* New York: Chelsea House, 1989.

Cantor, Aviva. "She Fought Back — An Interview with Vilna Partisan Vitke Kempner." *Lilith* 16 (Spring 1987): 20–24.

Dash, Joan. *Summoned to Jerusalem: The Life of Henrietta Szold.* New York: Harper & Row, 1979.

*Dash, Joan. *The Triumph of Discovery: Women Scientists Who Won the Nobel Prize.* Englewood Cliffs, N.J.: Julian Messner, 1991.

Encyclopedia Judaica. Jerusalem: Keter Publishing House, 1972.

Gerber, Jane. *The Jews of Spain: A History of the Sephardic Experience.* New York: Free Press, 1992.

Ginzberg, Louis. *Legends of the Jews.* Philadelphia: Jewish Publication Society, 1975.

Goldman, Emma. *Living My Life: An Autobiography of Emma Goldman.* Edited by Richard and Anna Maria Drinnon. New York: Meridian, 1977.

Grossman, Susan and Rivka Haut. *Daughters of the King: Women and the Synagogue.* Philadelphia: Jewish Publication Society, 1992.

Gutman, Israel, ed. *Encyclopedia of the Holocaust.* New York: MacMillan Publishing Co., 1990.

Hay, Peter. *Ordinary Heroes: Chana Szenes and the Dream of Zionism.* New York: Putnam, 1986.

Henry, Sondra and Emily Taitz. *Written Out of History: Our Jewish Foremothers.* New York: Biblio Press, 1990.

*Henry, Sondra and Emily Taitz. *Betty Friedan: Fighter for Women's Rights.* Hillside, N.J.: Enslow Publishers, 1990.

Hymowitz, Carol and Michaele Weissman. *A History of Women in America.* New York: Bantam Books, 1978.

Kessner, Carole S. *The "Other" New York Intellectuals.* New York: New York University Press, 1994.

Kohut, Rebekah. *More Yesterdays.* New York: Bloch Publishing Co., 1950.

Koltun, Elizabeth, ed. *The Jewish Woman: New Perspectives.* New York: Schocken, 1978.

Kuzmack, Linda Gordon. *Woman's Cause.* Columbus, Ohio: Ohio State University Press, 1990.

Lacks, Roslyn. *Women in Judaism: Myth, History, and Struggle.* Garden City, N.Y.: Doubleday & Co., 1980.

*Lefer, Diane. *Emma Lazarus.* New York: Chelsea House, 1988.

Levin, Alexander Lee. *The Szolds of Lombard Street.* Philadelphia: Jewish Publication Society, 1960.

Libeson, Anita Libman. *Recall to Life: Jewish Women in American History.* Cranbury, N.J.: Thomas Yoseloff, 1970.

Lisle, Laurie. *Louise Nevelson: A Passionate Life.* New York: Summit Books, 1990.

Lowenthal, Marvin, ed. and trans. *The Memoirs of Gluckl of Hameln.* New York: Schocken Books, 1977.

Mann, Peggy. *Golda: The Life of Israel's Prime Minister.* New York: Washington Square Press, 1973.

Roth, Cecil. *The House of Nasi: Dona Gracia.* Philadelphia: Jewish Publication Society, 1948.

Rubens, A. *Book of Jewish Costume.* New York: Crown Publishing, 1972.

*Siegel, Beatrice. *Lillian Wald of Henry Street.* New York: Macmillan Publishing Co., 1983.

*Suhl, Yuri. *Ernestine L. Rose, Women's Rights Pioneer.* New York: Biblio Press, 1990.

Umansky, Ellen and Dianne Ashton, eds. *Four Centuries of Jewish Women's Spirituality: A Sourcebook.* Boston: Beacon Press, 1992.

Wald, Lillian. *The House on Henry Street.* New York: Henry Holt, 1915.

*Waldstreicher, David. *Emma Goldman: A Biography.* New York: Chelsea House (American Women of Achievement Series), 1990.

Wexler, Alice. *Emma Goldman: An Intimate Life.* New York: Pantheon Books, 1989.

*Indicates juvenile or young adult books.

PHOTO & ILLUSTRATION ACKNOWLEDGMENTS

Eve, A pastel and gouache by Lucien Levy Dhurmer, 1896 (pp. ii, 4, 5, front cover).

Sarah, Old drawing by J. Matham after Golzius. Courtesy of the Metropolitian Museum of Art, The Elisha Whittlesey Collection, The Elisha Whittlesey Fund, 1951 (p. 6).

Rebecca, Etching by Gustave Doré (pp. ii, 7, 8, front cover).

Rachel, Etching by Gustave Doré (p. 9, 10).

Miriam, Etching by Edward Poynter, collection of Biblio Press (p. 11).

Deborah, Etching by Gustave Doré (pp. ii, 12, front cover).

Yael, Painting by Pellegrini (Venice, eighteenth century) (p. 13).

Ruth, Etching by Gustave Doré (p. 15).

Esther, Photo of section of a mural from the Dura Europa synagogue (third century) (p. 16).

Judith, From a painting by Tintoretto (Venice, sixteenth century) (pp. 18, 20).

Map of the Middle East and North Africa, Drawn by Emily Taitz (pp. ix, x, xi, 24, 26).

Young Ethiopian, Photo by Ruth Gruber, author of *Rescue: The Exodus of Ethiopian Jews* (p. 29).

Geniza room, New York Public Library Collection (pp. 30, 31).

Worms Synagogue, Old lithograph. New York Public Library Collection (pp. 36, 41).

Rebecca Polona title page, Courtesy of the Library of the Jewish Theological Seminary of America (pp. viii, 43).

Italian Jewish manuscript, Courtesy of the Library of the Jewish Theological Seminary of America (p. 44).

Early printing press, Old drawing. New York Public Library Collection (p. 47).

Renaissance women, The Israel Museum, Jerusalem (pp. 50, 51).

Map of Italy, Drawn by Emily Taitz (p. 56).

Dona Gracia Nasi, Jewish Museum/Art Resource, NY. S0068055 FB77 B&W Print. Medal of Gracia Nasi, the younger. Ferrara, 1558. By Pastorino di Giovan Michele de'Pastorini (c.1508-1592). Bronze, cast. 2 5/8 in. diam (6.6 cm). Gift of the Samuel and Daniel M. Friedenberg Collection, FB77. Jewish Museum, New York, U.S.A. (p. 59).

Map of Europe, Drawn by Emily Taitz (p. 64).

Maid of Ludomir, Copyright M. Ellner (p. 72).

Hasidic woman, Courtesy Isaac and Emily Taitz (p. 73).

Polish synagogue, Collection of Tel Aviv Museum of Art (pp. xiv, 78, 80).

Rachel Morpurgo, *Gallery of Hebrew Poets* (p. 84, 89).

Annie Nathan Meyer, Barnard College Archives (pp. ii, 96, 109, front cover).

Rebecca Gratz, Delaware Art Museum. Gift of Benjamin Shaw II (p. 98).

Penina Moise, Courtesy Solomon Breibart, Temple Beth Elohim, Charleston, S.C. (p. 100).

Ernestine Rose, Library of Congress, LC-USZ62-52045 (p. 103).

Emma Lazarus, Library of Congress, LC-USZ62-15241 (pp. ii, 105, front cover).

Bertha Pappenheim, Collection of Biblio Press (pp. 110, 116).

Sarah Schnirer, The YIVO Institute for Jewish Research (p. 113).

Lily Montagu, Private Collection, Ellen M. Umansky (p. 118).

Mathilde Schechter, Courtesy of the National Women's League for Conservative Judaism (p. 119).

Golda Meir, Courtesy of the Consulate General of Israel, NYC (p. 120); Stamp issued by the State of Israel to honor the memory of Golda Meir (pp. ii, 132, front cover).

Palestine pioneers, Collection of Biblio Press (p. 122).

Manya Shochat, Collection of Biblio Press (p. 126).

Henrietta Szold, Courtesy of Hadassah, the Woman's Zionist Organization of America, Inc. (pp. ii, 129, 130, front cover).

Lillian Wald, Courtesy Visiting Nurse Service of New York (pp. 134, 143).

Clara Lemlich, Catherwood Library, New York State School of Industrial and Labor Relations; Cornell University (p. 136).

Rose Schneiderman, Library of Congress, LC-USZ62-30358 (p. 138).

Emma Goldman, Library of Congress, LC-USZ62-42504 (p. 146).

Zivia Lubetkin, The YIVO Institute for Jewish Research (p. 151).

Vitke Kempner Kovner, The YIVO Institute for Jewish Research (pp. ii, 2, 148, 153, back cover).

Hannah Szenes, The YIVO Institute for Jewish Research (p. 159).

Bertha Kalich, Library of Congress, LC-USZ62-75177 (pp. ii, 2, 160, back cover).

Rosalyn S. Yalow, Ph.D., Senior Medical Investigator Emeritus, VA, Solomon A. Berson Distinguished Professor-at-Large Mount Sinai School of Medicine, CUNY, Nobel Laureate in Physiology or Medicine, 1977 (p. 163).

Louise Nevelson, 1968. Courtesy PaceWildenstein (p. 165).

Betty Friedan, Joyce Ravid photo for Touchstone Books (pp. ii, 167, front cover).

Ruth Bader Ginsburg, Collection, The Supreme Court Historical Society (pp. ii, 2, 170, back cover).

Judith Resnick, NASA (pp. ii, 172, front cover).

Women academics, Hilary Marcus/Impact Visuals (pp. 174, 176).

Judith Kaplan Eisenstein, Courtesy Judith Kaplan Eisenstein (p. 179).

Nehama Leibowitz, Courtesy Yitshak Reiner (p. 180).

Cynthia Ozick, Ricki Rosen photo for Alfred Knopf (p. 182).

Judith Hauptman, Photo by Abraham Menashe (pp. 2, 185, back cover).

Women praying, Courtesy Women's *Tefilah* of Great Neck, Rita Gordenson (p. 186).

Sally Preisand, Hebrew Union College (pp. ii, 2, 188, back cover).

Sandy Sasso, Photo by Larry Seidman (p. 191).

Amy Eilberg, Courtesy Rabbi Amy Eilberg (pp. ii, 2, 193, back cover).

Young women, Personal collection of Naomi Taitz (p. 197).

Index

Note: Page numbers in **bold face** indicate photographs, and page numbers in *italics* indicate illustrations.

216